© Claire Watts

Octavia Bright is a writer and broadcaster. She co-hosts *Literary Friction*, the literary podcast and NTS Radio show, with Carrie Plitt. Recommended by the *New York Times*, *Guardian*, BBC Culture, *Electric Literature*, *Sunday Times* and others, it has run for ten years and since 2016 has had over 1.4 million downloads. She has also presented programmes for BBC Radio 4 including *Open Book*, and hosts literary events for bookshops, publishers and festivals – such as Cheltenham Literature Festival and events for The Southbank Centre. Her writing has been published in a number of magazines including the *White Review*, *Harper's Bazaar*, *ELLE*, *Wasafiri*, *Somesuch Stories* and the *Sunday Times*, amongst others. She has a PhD from the Spanish department at UCL.

@octaviabright_ | octavia.bright

OCTAVIA BRIGHT

This Ragged Grace

A Memoir of Recovery & Renewal

CANONGATE

First published in Great Britain in 2023
by Canongate Books Ltd, 14 High Street, Edinburgh EH1 1TE

canongate.co.uk

1

British Library Cataloguing-in-Publication Data
A catalogue record for this book is available on
request from the British Library

ISBN 978 1 83885 746 2

Typeset in Bembo by Palimpsest Book Production Ltd,
Falkirk, Stirlingshire

Printed and bound in Great Britain by Clays Ltd, Elcograf S.p.A.

The spiral is an attempt at controlling the chaos. It has two directions. Where do you place yourself, at the periphery or at the vortex? Beginning at the outside is the fear of losing control; the winding in is a tightening, a retreating, a compacting to the point of disappearance. Beginning at the center is affirmation, the move outward is a representation of giving, and giving up control; of trust, positive energy, of life itself.

Louise Bourgeois

CONTENTS

PROLOGUE

I WALKED SO HARD AND SO fast in the winter of 2013 that I wore right through a pair of red Doc Martens. Things felt very raw and I was full of fear. I was OK standing still if I had voices in my ears, a podcast or an audiobook for company, but before long impatience would overwhelm me and I'd have to move my legs. My muscles propelled themselves and I found myself carried all over the city.

Even in my flat I struggled to be still. I made playlists of repetitive, upbeat music and in the evenings I would close the shutters and dance. Then I could forget myself, as if the movement were a spell, a way of escaping the things I wasn't ready to face. It felt like a compulsion, not a choice, like the luckless girl in *The Red Shoes* (my boots were the colour of oxblood so maybe there was something in it).

Seven months earlier I'd stopped drinking. It's funny how we say that, 'stopped drinking', as though the only liquid worth talking about is alcohol. Had I stopped drinking entirely I would have had about three days to live – not very long. Either way, I had stopped drinking alcohol at the end of a hot June at the beginning of a messy summer and by the time the days were shortening the pink cloud of new sobriety had worn off and I was unable to be still.

Between my last drink – a warm bottle of cheap white wine shared with a couple of friends on my sitting-room floor (had I known it would be my last I would have chosen something else, maybe a chilled tequila cocktail with salted grapefruit and lime) – and the first frost, I crossed the threshold into that superstitious realm: the age of twenty-seven. Most of the preceding year had been filled with chaos and blind, impulsive action, and it wasn't until I found myself aligned with this new number, bruised and sober, that its significance hit me: the so-called twenty-seven club, that roll-call of young artists who died in their twenty-eighth year whether by their own hand or in other tragic circumstances. I, of course, did not see myself as next in a line-up that includes Jimi Hendrix, Kurt Cobain, Janis Joplin, Jean-Michel Basquiat, Jim Morrison and Amy Winehouse, but it left me wondering about the tenderness of that stage of life, when one is adult but often not entirely, and when destructive habits are just starting to lose the glittering sheen of youthful folly.

My extended adolescence had abruptly reached its end.

The Descent

THE FIRST YEAR SOBER

If we go down into ourselves we find that we possess
exactly what we desire. – Simone Weil

THAT WINTER, ON TOP OF a teal metal bookcase in my
sitting room sat an odd collection of items. They were
arranged in a makeshift altar in front of which I had tried to
cultivate a daily meditation practice: a life-size plastic skull, painted
Yves Klein blue; incense, I don't remember which kind; a postcard with a drawing of a naked woman riding a winged horse
– a Russian tattoo design in a kitsch red frame given to me by
a school friend when I was sixteen; two dried pink roses in glass
vases; a print of Georgia O'Keeffe's painting *Summer Days*, in
which an animal skull is suspended against a cloudy sky above
a posy of desert flowers and a barren, red rock landscape beneath
– the skull's horns make the shape of a human pelvis, and in
the distance there's enough blue sky to make a sailor suit (a

phrase I hear in my mother's voice); three candles; and a much underlined copy of Simone Weil's *Gravity and Grace*.

Gravity and Grace is a compilation of writing by Weil, recommended to me by a friend when I told him I was getting sober. 'She'll make the Twelve Step theology more intellectual and mystic,' promised Steve, 'and she has some beautiful expressions on love.' Intellectual and mystic were two things I could get behind, and a French philosopher known as 'the patron saint of all outsiders' was a much more appealing spiritual guide than the little blue book I had dutifully purchased at an AA meeting. Sitting on a green metal folding chair in yet another church basement, I had leafed through its thin pages disappointed by how like a Bible it was, my heart sinking when I saw it had a chapter called 'To Wives'. I was not a wife, nor did I have one. Whereas with Weil, I was comforted by her confidence in the power of introspection – that going down into oneself can be a salve for the discontents of desire. But, when I did manage to go down into myself, often I found that I did not – as Simone promised – possess exactly what I desired. Instead I found that itch in my muscles that meant, for all my good intentions, I could not be still for long enough to discover much at all. *Gravity and Grace* is written in fragments, so my scattered mind only had to concentrate on a few lines at a time, but I was still too restless to really grasp what they were getting at. Still, each morning it was that introspection I strove for, in front of my altar, kneeling to prove that I meant it.

On the altar there was also a small glass jar of sand. Grey and volcanic, it came from the island of Stromboli, where I had gone with a close friend in August of that summer, when I was not quite twenty-seven and just a few weeks into this new, thirsty life. Everything there is covered in a black dust which Giovanna, the owner of our bed and breakfast, assured us was sterile, cooked in the mountain at 300 degrees.

Kate and I arrived in Ginostra by water taxi, a wooden motorboat powered by a local man named Frank – gruff voice, wide grin, strong hands – who we met at the main port. There are no cars on the island, and you can't reach the tiny settlement (a former fishing village) any other way. Almost unbearable joy pulsed through me as salty air blew my hair across my face and we buffeted against the crests of perfectly formed little waves. The water was the deepest blue, many shades darker than the skull on my altar, and dense as velvet.

The postman on Stromboli was a stringy German man with silver hair and two donkeys who carried the parcels and letters up the island's steep, zig-zagging paths. Their saddles were fitted with panniers in the blue and yellow livery of the Italian postal service, and we soon discovered that they did not like being stroked while they were at work. We heard a rumour that the German postman's wife was a philosopher who had studied with Theodor Adorno, a fact I found romantic because I had encountered his work during my Master's, though beyond the fact he was against capitalism, all I really remembered was that he looked like a serious, bespectacled egg. At the time, I made a point of looking up the photographs of every male philosopher and cultural critic on the course, fed up that men could be known for their ideas alone while women were mostly known by their bodies first.

How romantic, I thought, to live here on the edge of this active volcano with a brain full of anti-capitalist philosophy. How free they must be. Imagine a life not governed by mindless consumption. Perhaps living in Ginostra meant you could almost escape it altogether – there are no billboards, no advertisements. There are two little shops, one where you can buy dried things – capers, olives and tinned tomatoes, pasta, onions and bread – and one that sells fresh produce which comes in with the boats, and is therefore less reliable. Nearby there is a church, outside which there is a terrace where everyone gathers to watch the sunset and share an *aperitivo* in the evenings. Up the hill, a couple of restaurants. Not much else.

It was on that terrace outside the church, with the sun hanging orange and low in the sky, that I got talking to a French woman named Fleur. A journalist who had been covering the migration crisis in the Mediterranean for a French news agency, she had been coming to Stromboli to decompress for several years. I don't know how it happened but we soon found we were talking about love. She used the word 'lover' with a sincerity I admired, certain I could never pull it off. But Fleur's lovers were not satisfying her. In fact what she was telling me was a story of deep dissatisfaction, of an unfillable void, which was a story I knew well.

I love it here, she told me in her soft voice, it's so calm. Yes, I agreed, it is so calm here at the foot of an active volcano.

I wondered if Fleur and I were desert flowers that could only flourish under arid conditions.

I felt safe in the shadow of that elemental danger, held fast in the heat and sheltered by hot pink bougainvillea. For a few sweet days, the past stopped existing. But I knew that it was not acceptable to only be able to flourish on holiday.

Adjusting the straps of her top, Fleur told me there was a man on the island who she slept with on her last stay. She wasn't sure where things stood but she would like to find out if they could do it again. He intrigued her, she said. The German with the post donkeys climbed past us up the path. The donkeys had strapped to them the catch of the day and two generous boxes of oranges and I watched them go, hooked on the scent of the fruit that carried in the heat. Before she left me I asked Fleur if she knew about the postman's philosopher wife who had studied under Adorno. Yes, she said, I heard that too, apparently she has beautiful white hair.

As she cast off in search of her would-be lover, I mentally wished her a satisfying time. I stayed on the terrace, watched the orange and pink sunset deepen then fade as the bright disc of sun slipped down behind the sea. That night on the island, the sky was so thick with celestial bodies it felt like I could see the whole universe.

The truth was that the philosophy of Adorno wasn't the only thing I'd forgotten: my brain felt increasingly full of holes. I'd come to picture it like an old ruin – walls mostly still standing but no roof to speak of and windows blown out a long time ago. That night on Stromboli, by the light of the Milky Way, I found myself fascinated by the idea of this woman, this white-haired, island-dwelling philosopher. I imagined her striding up the sides of the volcano each morning, strong and tanned, note-book in hand. I wanted to know her.

In my fantasy, the logic of lava flows inspired her work, most notably her theory of sovereignty, which believed that the dynamic potential of emotion could advance the greater needs of the collective: there is no volcano without lava; there is no whole without its parts. She'd say, it's not solipsism to pay attention to your interior world – if you don't you're guaranteed to be surprised by an eruption. I imagined she wore a strand of volcanic glass beads long enough to wrap twice around her neck, and ate garlicky prawns at candlelit dinners under the intricate Aeolian night sky. Hers was a life of glamorous simplicity, reading and writing books, sending letters, feeding the donkeys.

When I found out that Dolce & Gabbana owned a villa on the island, the dream of my anti-capitalist utopia stretched to accommodate the new information. I found photographs of it online – in keeping with the other buildings there, it had a white-washed exterior but inside was, as per their famous aesthetic, a riot of colour and texture, gilded mirrors and glossy tiles. So now there were also D&G dresses in the philosopher's repertoire (in my mind they were generous friends to her), and, occasionally, glitzy parties. The life I imagined for her looked more and more like a Pedro Almodóvar film: stylish and beautifully appointed, full of humour. My imaginary philosopher enjoyed her life but never overdid it, allowed herself pleasure but was never a slave to it. I began to see that she had come to Stromboli to live out her inconsistencies in relative peace, and I envied her. My own inconsistencies had run me ragged – I was ready for some relief.

Only then did I understand that the glamorous philosopher who was married to the stringy German postman was a cipher for my deep need to feel sovereign myself. I'd been in thrall to my habits for too long, and it was not a free life. Addiction drags you away from reality, that's why at first it feels so good, or at least like temporary respite. And isn't it a very human thing, to want to feel good? But I was finally ready to disentangle myself from a set of beliefs I had unconsciously absorbed, theories of pleasure and intellect, femininity and abandon, identity and behaviour, structures I had unwittingly adopted as simply how to be. I had sought to feel glamorous, dangerous, liberated; these were the things I had wanted, but they were costumes I put on, and I'd grown attached to the story of my chaos. Now I was trying a new way, a more conscious way. A path of greater self-determination.

And so it was there, in the Mediterranean heat, in the shadow of an elemental chaos so much bigger than my own, that I first surrendered to the idea of recovery.

The next day, with the sunlight clean and strong on my limbs, I lay back and let the clear, salty water fill my ears. All I could hear was my heartbeat. Slow. I felt the rumble of the volcano beneath me. Floating, my body motionless but for the gentle rise and fall made by tiny cerulean waves.

No man is an island, sure, but a person can feel like a sleepy volcano in the middle of the Tyrrhenian Sea.

Except Stromboli is far from dormant. Fountains of molten rock periodically jet into the sky, and from our vantage point at its base Kate and I marvelled at the puffs of grey smoke that were occasionally visible as they mingled with fluffy clouds drifting past above. Before long we grew used to it, as we discovered the strange paradox of volcano life – sitting naked on the island's hot black rocks under my wide-brimmed sun hat I smoked a cigarette and felt at peace, completely unable to connect those emissions with any real sense of threat. Not once did I worry for our safety.

(Five years after we happily gave ourselves over to the island's lazy rhythms, Mount Stromboli had a serious eruption. It claimed the life of one hiker and sent a hot blast of ash and smoke a mile into the sky and several hundred metres into the sea. I read about it in *Time* magazine and *National Geographic*, and sent the articles to Kate in messages full of exclamation marks: *I can't believe she blew her top!!! I hope the donkeys are OK . . . that poor hiker – what a way to go.*)

The volcanic dust continued to work its way under the nails of my fingers and toes and I relaxed. Gave myself over to the start and end of each day, as it's impossible not to do on an island of that size; the sky is bigger than the land on which you stand. It was a relief to be so far from London and the temptations I was trying to leave behind. Here, I was surrounded by symbols of renewal – not just the tidal ebbs and flows, the sunrise and sunset, but the volcano itself, constantly ejecting fragments of its own matter, always growing, purging, consuming. An ancient paradox, constant yet constantly changing. It filled me with optimism.

I thought about the lava, how over the years it has bubbled up from seething depths and torn a raw path across the mountain's surface like a wound, known as the Sciara del Fuoco, or scree of fire. The incandescent waste tumbles down the north flank of the volcano, where it has healed into a blackened scar. Destruction and creation. Rupture and renewal.

The eponymous trip in Jules Verne's novel *Journey to the Centre of the Earth* concludes on the slopes of Mount Stromboli. Riding an explosive lava flow to the surface, Professor Lidenbrock, his nephew Axel and their guide Hans emerge from the centre of a volcano they are surprised to discover is not the dormant Icelandic one through which they had originally descended. Tired, hungry, their clothes in tatters, they walk down, careful not to trip over hot debris, until they are met by the halcyon sight of olive trees, pomegranates and grapes on the vine. They help themselves to the restorative sweet fruit and can't believe their luck. It's an allegory of self-discovery: this scene on Stromboli is a moment of redemption and reward after the treacherous journey they've just survived, where they encountered prehistoric creatures, an unruly, underground sea, a looming giant. Scattered bones. They return changed, better integrated, having shed some of their old ideas and nurturing new ones.

What if the nephew, Axel, was so captivated by the island that he never left and took up life as the local postman? To look at the German with his donkeys (and supposedly a philosopher wife), in his vest and shorts, his worn sandals, you wouldn't know that he possessed the deepest secrets from the centre of the Earth, but it's quite possible that he does.

What I like about Verne's story is its wrong turns and misdirections. They don't know the route from the start. They have to change their minds and double back. In his vision, the centre of the Earth is full of evolutionary relics, dinosaurs and strange fish long extinct from the planet's surface. I like this idea that as we evolve, somewhere deep within us remains a skeletal trace of what came before that builds up in layers, a sediment of the self. But the point is that it's crucial to our continued survival to let some things sink to the bottom, recede until they are obsolete.

It's OK not to know where you're going. Course correction is a vital part of navigation. Knowledge and ignorance are bound together, the second being an initial condition of the first. There's a deep freedom in being able to change your mind.

Before I walked the paths on Stromboli – in the footprints of Lidenbrock, Axel and Hans – I did not know that capers are the buds of astonishingly beautiful flowers. *Capparis spinosa* thrives on the island, happily growing in the loamy volcanic soil (Spinoza, another philosopher whose work I'd forgotten, but whose romantic black curls were seared into my memory – his scalp was as luscious as Adorno's was bald). The white blooms were everywhere that August, glowing in the flat, bright light. I was captivated by their large petals, pale, occasionally a little pink, and how they set off the clusters of long, purple stamens that exploded from their centre. An echo of the volcanic fireworks that shoot out of Mount Stromboli itself. The stamens gave each flower a busy violet halo that bounced, chaotic, in the breeze, and their scent was warm and sweet.

I couldn't stop thinking of these extravagant flowers as I chased several of their tight, green buds around my plate with a fork, the night we had dinner at the restaurant up the hill. ('The new restaurant', Giovanna had called it, with more than a little suspicion in her voice.) After a perilous, pitch-dark scramble along an eventually candlelit path, I felt my senses heightened, pupils fully dilated. The briny flavour of my *spaghetti alla strombolana* was sharp on my tongue. Did you know that capers are harvested each morning before they can blossom into flowers? I asked Kate, picturing the blousy ornaments of their blooms. I was proud of my new fact. She seemed to know it already. Nipped in the bud, I thought to myself.

We had been talking about love over a plate of grilled prawns. Why am I always talking about love? I thought. I wanted to be a more serious person, with a brain full of Adorno and Spinoza, worthy of the doctorate I was working towards, but instead all I could think about was love, love, love. I looked at the prawns, their armoured bodies curled against one another, spooning, and remembered that lobsters famously mate for life. Going by the scene on the plate in front of me, prawns were more into sharing. My mind tumbled down the path of a polyamorous crustaceous romance as I cracked the next creature's shell to get at its sweet flesh. Sounds fun, I thought, and sucked out its brains. All that love.

Sometimes it feels good to lose your head to love. What bliss to get lost in another person's body, and consciousness – those early weeks and months when all that matters is the one you've fallen for, what they think, the smell of their neck, when you'll see them next. The feeling in your guts when the letters of their name light up the screen of your phone. The glorious challenge of their otherness, and the deepening pleasure of all the ways in which you are the same.

But I was also coming to see that love, like drinking, had become another way for me to lose myself completely. I placed the prawn's head, empty now, on my side plate which piled ever higher with the remains of its fallen comrades.

Is it really love at all, if at its heart it's another way to escape yourself, just another fix? I asked Kate, who lived life always a few steps ahead of me, which was one of the reasons I loved her.

It's a good question, she said, passing me the finger bowl of lemony water. Does it matter? There are many different kinds of love. Just because something ended up not being good for you, doesn't mean you should write it off completely. It's all experience.

She was getting at something important that I didn't want to hear. Here on Stromboli I felt light and open, but I knew that since stopping drinking my thoughts had started to arrange themselves into more binary categories: right and wrong, good and bad, safe and dangerous. It was to do with fear. I felt too fragile to live in the grey area, still uncertain in my choice. Ambivalence is a hard feeling to bear. Also, a love that had gone bad was not long in the past and I needed it to stay that way – extricating myself had been the precursor to choosing a different kind of life.

It had been a classic first love. To begin with it burned heady bright, wheels greased by whiskey and heavy guitars in my narrow university halls bedroom. We kept it intense and dramatic as we went on to live in different cities, then different countries. We made desperate late-night phone calls from flimsy booths in internet cafes, our feelings stoked by the brutality of our phonecards running out. We took long bus trips across Europe by night, arriving at dawn, tender and full of longing, relief at the sight of each other's faces utterly intoxicating. The feelings were oceanic, they came in waves to drown everything else out. In that, there was solace, but underneath something festered.

Before, I had written daily in notebooks where I would try to digest the world around me, make sense of myself and imagine what other excitement life might hold. But after falling into this world of feeling, instead of thinking about my future I figured I could just *be in love*. I gave myself over to it completely, and for a while it was everything – too much – but it was good. Soon, it calcified into dependence, into need, the way that any addiction does. It became something that held us both in stasis, specimens in a jar labelled 'first try', suspended by our codependence. Part of me knew this before I understood it, and it was this knowledge that slowly swelled into courage enough to end it, in spite of the feeling that I was also breaking my own heart.

I picked up a charred lemon slice from the now almost empty plate of prawns and bit off the tart triangles of its segments one by one. It was sweeter than I'd expected, the sugar lightly cara-melised by the grill. I think I need to take a break from all of it, I said, not yet sure if I meant it.

The best of love makes you focused on the needs of the other, open, generous and curious, but fixating on love is the opposite of that – it's all about meeting your own urgent want, immediately and at all costs, so as to block any intolerable feeling or tune out a reality that seems unbearable. Used this way, I learned that romance can be just another form of consumption. It's why addicts tend to make such intense and beguiling lovers, at least at first: in a way, our survival comes to depend on it.

I was reminded of some lines from *Gravity and Grace* that I'd written in my notebook before going away:

Love needs reality. What is more terrible than the discovery that through a bodily appearance we have been loving an imaginary being.

Steve was right, Weil was good on love, but I couldn't yet find beauty in this fragment because it hit too close to home. It felt more like taking medicine, and without a spoonful of sugar to help it go down.

Love needs reality. Reality was not a place I often wanted to be, especially not when I was in love – the whole point of it was to escape the everyday. But love had often ended up feeling inadequate, and I was beginning to understand why. I'd thought it was because I simply wanted too much, that maybe it was time to learn how to want less, but I was slowly starting to see it was actually about learning to want something altogether different. If love was to be more than a fix, it had to be the kind that could withstand reality, not the kind that needs to escape it to survive. Like the deep love I felt for my friends, which made room for disappointment and change as well as the pleasure of feeling understood.

Kate and I finished eating and sat, smoking in the candlelight, looking at the moon's reflection dancing on the sea. I only smoke when I'm in Europe, she said, taking a drag on a Camel blue.

It made me smile because it seemed we'd come all this way just to smoke American cigarettes. The volcano rumbled and puffed out a thin thread of dust, right on cue.

But what of the glamorous philosopher and her charmed island life? Did she live in reality, or had she come here to escape it? Already, I wanted to come back to Stromboli before I'd even left, but I knew if I tried to stay it would be an attempt to turn a parenthesis into a full sentence, or even a whole book. Only a few hundred people live on the island full time. A violent eruption in 1930 killed six and shrank the population down from 5,000 as islanders fled in search of a less precarious place to build their homes. For those that remain, summer is a time of invasion, as people like me come in search of escape, starlight, or the volcano's ancient wisdom. Day-trippers, paradise hunters. We ought to bring it and its inhabitants something in return, besides our money. Something of equal value.

I also knew it wouldn't be long before the itch returned – I doubted I'd survive without the distractions of city life. For a few days, maybe even weeks, I could fill my emptiness with the ashen sand, the swell of stars and the tales of other people's lovers, but eventually it wouldn't be enough. Nothing ever was.

And what of the philosopher's love for the postman, who might as well be the boy who never left? It was a love without possession, I decided to myself, open and strong. Its foundations were respect and curiosity, not hunger and need. I idealised it completely.

The following morning, among the bobbing heads of caper flowers, I fantasised about discovering her notebooks (which, unlike me, she hadn't stopped writing in when she'd fallen in love). I imagined she'd left them on a flat black rock at the water's edge – there were three of them, each bound in a different shade of green. The top one had fallen open, and with a tremor of guilt in my fingers I lifted it up, smoothing down the page to read:

It's not just the buds of capers that are worth knowing about – the plant's fruit is the caper berry, an elegant, plump tear drop on a thick stalk, also generally served pickled. In the Bible (Ecclesiastes 12:5, to be precise), depending on which translation from the Hebrew you trust, caper berries are a symbol of desire and an aphrodisiac. If you split open the smooth green surface of a caper berry you find a frenzy of little seeds inside, tightly packed, like a pomegranate.

The seeds of many different desires and possibilities, I thought, pickled out of their potential. As I wrote some lines about the capers in my own little green notebook, I began to see myself this way too, as a person thwarted by a substance that halted my progress and cut me off from growth.

The spring before I went to Stromboli, in May 2013, when I was still drinking, I had a motorbike accident. It left me with dark bruises and an impressive road burn up the back of my right calf and thigh. It required the kind of recovery that involves hospitals and bandages and lying down, the kind you can't argue with. I told my parents I'd 'fallen off a bike' and avoided them until it all looked less dramatic, but something had finally happened that I couldn't shrink for myself.

The accident also happened in Italy, but in Milan. I had just handed in the first chapter of my thesis, and was visiting a friend who lived there to celebrate her birthday. It had been a hard year, and the chapter was a hot mess, but I didn't know that yet and was flying high on meeting the deadline. We danced, we drank, we ate truffle *piadinas*, strung balloons up in the park giggling barefoot on the grass. Late one night I made a reckless decision and got on the back of a man's white Yamaha in my flimsy sundress and woven shoes. He wore leathers. We were strangers to one another and neither of us were sober. When in a sharp turn we met a light rain, the bike swung out from under us resulting in his bruised ribs, a slight concussion each and my road burn. It scorched down my leg, livid and raw.

In the emergency room the nurses cleaned my wounds with impressive efficiency, removing all traces of the abrasive grit and tarmac that had worked their way into me as I slid across the road. They mended me with a webbing that encourages rapid skin growth and then eventually dissolves, leaving the new skin intact: a broken doll, glued back together. They told me I was lucky not to need a skin graft. Through the haze of the gas and air I imagined the nurses were enchanted and their hands were made of soothing ice. They swaddled me in white bandages from ankle to hip, gave me some crutches, and sent me on my way. Once I was back in London and the dressings could be removed, I was given strict instructions to rub everything with Vitamin E oil each day to prevent scarring, which I did religiously. More religiously than I have ever been able to kneel at my altar in pursuit of serenity. Vanity is a stronger motivator than peace.

It hurt, and later frightened me, but the truth is I loved the speed of the bike in the dark. It was intoxicating. Finally, I was moving fast enough to outrun myself, and I forgot myself completely. Forgot everything, even my body. Motion can be liberation, at least for a few swift minutes. The same can be said of risk: the thrill of the jumping-off point eclipses all other feeling, and in that moment you are free from yourself, made only of anticipation and desire.

Writing this now, I think of Mary Gaitskill's essay *Lost Cat* which is about love, loss and the complexities of intimacy, where she writes, 'it is hard to protect a person you love from pain, because people often choose pain; *I* am a person who often chooses pain'. Though pain was certainly where I ended up that night, it wasn't what I thought I was choosing. Abandon was what I wanted, which is not necessarily the same. And compulsion never feels like choice at the time. In truth, I longed to be lost to myself. I was looking for the void, which I could only face with a sideways glance or by hurtling towards it at reckless speed. On, say, a shining white Yamaha.

What does it mean if abandon is your pleasure? I've always found a thrill in leaving the vessel of my body, in abandoning ship. It can be exhausting to be a person in a body. And if you seek the feeling of leaving that body momentarily, forgetting its fragility and its mortality, beneath the pleasure of the thrill, is it really pain you're after, or is it something else? I kept putting myself in danger, and I couldn't make it stop. It's only the death drive, my dear, Freud would likely tell me, if I laid my body down on his carpet-covered couch. Everyone needs a little oblivion from time to time. Besides, what is the fantasy of the knight on a white charger if not an abandonment wish? A desire to be rescued from your own life by a story. And it's easier than you might think to use people as objects. A motorbike can be a tool; a knight also.

Of course, motorbikes promise certain things: speed, freedom, power. The fantasy of independence. That night, what I desired was to be suspended out of time, somewhere beyond all that was limited and unsatisfactory. I wanted a way out of my fate as a human animal with a body that had needs, with a life that needed tending to, the mundanity of it all. Maybe I was playing at symbolic masculinity, too. Borrowing it, trying it on for size – the motorbike as detachable phallus: a fallacy. Simone Weil says, 'we have to go down into the root of our desires in order to tear the energy from its object'. Simone says the object is not the point. The motorbike is pure energy, but it's not the point. The death drive will simply find another agent for its chaos.

Once home I struggled to be patient as my skin took its time to heal. The sticky ritual of the Vitamin E oil topped and tailed my days. The man I was seeing then helped me put it on, and told me I was a beautiful mess, which at the time I heard as a compliment. There was a lot of sitting still. I waited. One morning I woke to the insistent buzzing of flies. Unnerved, I tried to find where they were coming from, and couldn't. I wondered if I was being paranoid but the following day there were more of them, and by the evening I was worried. When daylight came I tried again to find the source and decided they had to be coming from a hatch that opened into the roof space – it looked like the rectangle of MDF fitted well enough but it was the only feasible answer. I couldn't climb a ladder to investigate because of my leg, so Pest Control sent a man named Lewis to come and have a look. His watery eyes were curious and shy, and his chin-length, mouse-coloured hair framed a pointed nose. He liked to crack jokes. I held the ladder for him and watched as his top half disappeared into the ceiling. As he reached for something up there, grunting slightly, his polo shirt rode up and I caught a glimpse of a bellybutton piercing, two pink gems catching the light, nestled in the centre of his soft torso. It's completely decomposed! he called down, thrilled. A squirrel had got in and died up there, the poor creature now stripped to its bones by the maggots that became the flies that I had not imagined after all.

I spent the afternoon googling decomposition, and felt somehow responsible for the animal's slow demise, as though my healing had required a flesh sacrifice.

By the time Kate and I disembarked from the hydrofoil onto Stromboli's black volcanic sands, my wounds – the visible ones, at least – had completely healed. In certain lights the new skin had a silvery sheen to it, and I was left with three dark stripes just below my right buttock that made it look like I'd survived a swipe from a big cat. Other than that, I was intact.

★   ★   ★

Every story you tell about yourself is an attempt to organise the messy experience of living. To map it out and put things in order can be a comfort – a day starts and ends, a year, a relationship, a habit. A descent. If you consider yourself an alcoholic, the story you are telling yourself is often about shame. It's easy to end it there, in that roiling, subterranean sea. But the voyage requires something more of you, and if you actually get into the sea of shame you get further down towards the root of your desires – you sink beneath the objects they fixate on, where you eventually find the truth. The motorbike is not the point. The alcohol is not the point. The accident was a moment of course correction precisely because I was already in up to my armpits.

The reason I had stopped drinking that June was because a psychiatrist had told me I was probably an alcoholic. Recovery was not my idea, and at first I did not particularly want it. I knew I drank habitually, but I felt that things hadn't yet got messy enough to warrant the exaggerated language he insisted on using: alcoholic, alcoholism, Alcoholics Anonymous.

But some ideas lay their roots in parts of the self that are just out of the ego's reach, and so you could also say that recovery *was* my idea, I just couldn't see it yet.

After all, it was me that had set off the chain of events that led me to the black leather chair in the psychiatrist's office. I had chosen to extricate myself from that long and intense first love, with all its drama. Spiralling, I had gone to Student Psychological Services for help and started seeing a therapist, and later, as I felt myself unravelling further, the psychiatrist. I had sat in the bright, warm sunlight that filled his airy room and explained that for a long time I had been having trouble sleeping. I could no longer distinguish my bedroom's night-time shadows from the figures erupting from my subconscious in the few moments of sleep I did manage to snatch. I cried often, felt overwhelmed by small tasks, and struggled to make sense of my academic work. I no longer found joy in the places I used to reliably seek it – nothing particularly unusual, just flowers and music, dancing, looking at art. I knew I was not well and I wanted to get better. To recover, if you will, though I did not yet understand from what.

The recovery I sought was a definitive, one-time thing, a problem he would quickly solve with a prescription and a diagnosis. Like getting over a stomach bug or bad flu: take a little pill, read a little book, get well again.

I sat back against the warm skin of the chair he offered me and noticed the cards pinned above his desk. They included a drawing by a small child and many colourful notes of thanks. The psychiatrist was an elderly man with large, kind eyes and a voice like David Attenborough's; he had worked with the university for a long time. Depressed PhD students were his speciality. After telling him everything I thought was wrong, I listened as he explained, gentle but firm, You are suffering from depression, anxiety and feelings of instability. He said these words with no trace of alarm, which calmed me. Writing out a prescription for an antidepressant, he looked at me over his glasses. You feel restless, irritable and discontent? I nodded. I see. I also think, he said, you have a drinking problem. The good news is, if you stop drinking, you can recover. He recommended a book about the addictive personality and asked me to attend three recovery meetings before our next appointment. His strong advice was not to say anything, just listen, and he told me the wisdom of recovering addicts and alcoholics was a precious resource.

Drinking was not something I remembered telling him about, in my tense and weepy litany of the things with which I struggled. I was blindsided by his words, though too proud to let on quite how much. I said thank you as I took the prescription from him, the word 'alcoholic' ringing loud in my ears. I didn't like it at all. I felt judged, though I later came to see the judgement was my own.

At first all I could see was restriction and denial, a life devoid of freedom or pleasure. Emptiness stretched out before me.

In *Gravity and Grace* there is a chapter called 'To Accept the Void', and when later I came to read it I thought back to that first meeting with the psychiatrist, and to his diagnosis. With his kind and patient smile he was asking me to accept the void. Only then would I be able to escape the grip it had on me. But back then the void wasn't something I wanted to accept, because acceptance meant knowing, and mystery was important to me. If it remained a nebulous thing that made life hard to live then who could blame any of us for seeking a little relief? Getting to know my void would mean taking responsibility for it, which was not very appealing. Weil says that in order to accept the void, 'a time has to be gone through without any reward, natural or supernatural'. But I like rewards, especially after doing something hard, like giving up drinking.

To begin with, the natural rewards were fairly immediate: the self-congratulatory feeling of sticking to something; my skin cleared up, got brighter; mornings were no longer intolerable or filled with dread. I remembered how to wake up, rather than come round. My concentration improved, meaning my work on my thesis was less frantic and haphazard, more methodical.

Then came the material things – for a while, like a good child of capitalism, I enjoyed attempting to fill my void with clothes for a life I was not actually living, vintage party dresses and high-heeled shoes, things I did not plan to wear to the library. On eBay I found a pair of electric blue and silver snakeskin platforms that had never been worn, and when I won the auction it felt like a sign from the universe that I was on the right track. They arrived and immediately I put them on, ignoring how they pinched at the sides. I could barely stand in them but I persevered because I felt I deserved them and also I was superstitious (super-stition is an excellent mask for fear): the shoes were an optimistic commitment to the parties of the future, when I would once again be able to drink. Because what I desired was not actually recovery. A chance to gather myself, maybe, but what I really desired was redemption, absolution for the unruly behaviour that had draped shame around my shoulders like a sodden velvet cape, heavy and unwanted. I had no intention, then, of accepting the void. Instead, that August I went to Stromboli.

But by the time the days were short and gloomy and I arrived and left the library in the dark, the rewards were further and fewer between, and the void was at my heels every hour of the day. Stromboli was an alternate reality. Perhaps a version of myself remained there, sun-bronzed and serene at the water's edge, her feet in the sea, but I was here in the slate-grey cold and my heart was heavy with angst. The story I was telling myself that restless low-sky winter was that it had become intolerable to be alone inside my mind and body without the substances I'd used to mitigate my experience of myself and the world.

Without them, I found that I was restless, and also that I was not alone. There was me, and then there was another relentless, awful voice. It was constant. An unremitting commentary on everything I did, everything I thought. An insidious, honeyed whisper laden with criticism and shame, but canny – it knew how to appeal to me, to my vanity. Sometimes it would cajole me, sometimes insult me, sometimes tease. It felt at once alien and a deep part of myself. All the miles I covered in those dark and fragile months were a desperate attempt to outrun it. I named it Wormtongue, after Tolkien's famous sycophant, and gave his voice a sound – wheedling, nasal. I made him Other, then tried to expel him.

Looking for a spell to silence him, I enrolled in a meditation course at the university. I wanted to descend down into myself so deep that I passed by him, so that I could then eject him from me in an explosion of lava and fiery ash. Every Monday at 9 a.m. I arrived back at Student Psychological Services and sat on the blue-carpeted floor of a big-windowed, white room along with eight or nine others, our winter coats in a large pile by the door. We were all PhD students with anxious eyes and tense jaws. Our teacher was a Buddhist but assured us that his guidance over the term would be secular. He seemed very kind and perhaps a little sad – *tristesse* was the word that came to mind. Somehow sorrow felt nobler in French.

In our first session he gave us this advice: don't talk about your meditation practice until you've been doing it for a few years. Most people meditate a handful of times then spend more time telling other people to try it than they do practising themselves.

There was a lesson in there about ego but Wormtongue was rustling too loudly for me to hear it. *We should go back to Paris*, he was saying, *we had fun in Paris*. Stop, I replied. You know I wasn't well there. *Whatever you say, doc. It was fun and you can't deny it. Besides, you're the one who was thinking about tristesse.*

On arrival the next Monday our teacher gave us each a custard cream. Judging by the reactions of the others in the room, it was only me who regularly ate biscuits for breakfast. They received theirs with reverence and curiosity, while I went to put mine straight in my mouth. Wait, said the teacher, not yet, not yet, as I fumbled with the biscuit and felt a hot blush flourish over my nose and across my cheeks.

Greedy guts, Wormtongue said. *Close that big, messy mouth.*

Our teacher explained we were to try an exercise in meditative eating. Behold the biscuit, he said. Turn it over in your hands. Take in every millimetre, every ridge. What's the texture like? And the smell? Breathe it in. Go slow, there's no hurry. I was longing to eat it but I did as he said, examined the sand-coloured rectangle with my eyes, my fingers, noticed the little cushion of sweet white cream sandwiched between the two outer biscuits, followed their raised, swirling pattern, traced the words 'custard' and 'cream' with the tip of my forefinger. I breathed in its scent – sugary, sickly – and waited for permission to put it in my mouth.

Take a taste of the biscuit, said our teacher. Pay attention to the texture and the flavour. I bit off a modest corner, enjoyed the crunch then crumble of sweet and salty matter and felt a tiny rush as the sugar melted on my tongue.

Wormtongue said: *More*.

More was what I wanted. I looked around at my fellow meditators and saw them all restrained and thoughtful, nibbling delicately, eyes closed, brows furrowed into tiny erudite frowns as though tasting a fine wine. They were absorbed in the moment, entirely consumed with biscuit-tasting, which was the point of the exercise: presence through sensation. But Wormtongue and I were already lost to our craving for more. Furtive, I took another bite. I waited for an exquisite pleasure to invade my senses, like Proust and his interminable madeleine. I found nothing but irritation. It appeared like a pressure behind the eyes, ran down my neck, arms, fingers, churned in my stomach. More. *The Disease of More*, I'd heard it called, and knew that I had it. I wanted to be transported by the poetry of the custard cream to some higher plane of feeling and felt impatient for my own involuntary memory to strike, and elevate me – my love of biscuits came from my father, who had once worked for a biscuit company, which meant in my childhood the house had been full of biscuits, my uncle even had two ginger tomcats called The Ginger Biscuits; there must be hundreds of dormant biscuit-related memories waiting to be triggered by the scent and flavour. But craving blots everything else out. Nothing makes me feel so mortal as the feeling of more.

Powerless, I put the rest of the biscuit in my mouth.

I found the descent into myself to be painful and hard. In our third session I lay on my back on the blue carpet wishing I were floating instead in the Tyrrhenian Sea and tried to follow the Buddhist's voice as he counted our breaths in and out. It was a nice voice, gentle and steady. One, two, one, two. *One, two, buckle my shoe*, said Wormtongue. My skin itched, teeth wriggled in my mouth, toes clenched. Take balanced, even breaths, said the teacher, equal counts on the inhale and the exhale, and we'll meditate together for the next ten minutes. I kept breathing, one, two, one, two. The sounds slowed into abstractions, like the lowing of a field of cows, and my body began to ache. I let my eyes close. In the darkness I felt I was moving fast. An image came into focus: a woman and man on a motorbike, seen from above. The bare skin of her legs glowed amber, picked out against the night by each passing streetlamp. Her green dress fluttered against the bike's metalwork, its movement increasingly frantic as the machine gathered speed. Droplets of water began to fill the air as rain came and they leant into a right-hand turn. The road straightened out but the bike kept on leaning and their bodies were tossed across the tarmac like dice. Limbs flung in odd directions, they made awkward shapes on the ground as the bike came to a halt on its side between them, dumb wheels spinning the air.

I felt the nerves of my healed leg wound pulse to the steady beat of my heart. A deep pain in my right shoulder welled up into consciousness. Intense, like heat, and hard to bear. I opened my eyes, shifted my body. I sat up and rubbed at the site of the pain. It didn't help. Embarrassed at failing this simple task I explained to the teacher that I'd not long ago had an accident and was 'experiencing some discomfort'. Not my words, a politician's words, the words of a leaflet in a doctor's surgery or stamped on the back of an ointment.

I didn't want to tell him. It is very dull to be a broken thing.

Three, four, knock at the door, said Wormtongue. The knock of pain is boring but insistent. Wormtongue and I decided to let it in as we listened to our teacher explain how trauma held by the body can be hidden by the mind.

This was something I was supposed to know about. At the time, my days were spent in the British Library, where I sat in Humanities One obscured by an enormous pile of books about hysteria. Three of these books were very old and filled with dozens of photographs of women's bodies, all supposedly misbehaving. They were taken at the Salpêtrière Hospital in nineteenth-century Paris, where the women were patients or specimens, depending on how you looked at it. Some were twisted into strange poses, backs arched and fingers curled. Others looked completely ordinary, but their pictures were captioned with words like 'delirium', 'malingering' and 'melancholia'. From the safety of the reading room I read and read about the troubled history of this mystifying body language. I read about the invention of hysteria, the invention of psychoanalysis, the invention of trauma theory – pages and pages about bodies speaking dormant truths and the people (men) who tried to interpret them. It moved me. When not reading, I walked. The irony was, I walked and read so much that I tuned the language of my own body right out.

Drinking had done that too – made my body language incomprehensible, or simply drowned it in other sounds, other sensations. Now, I understand that a body which keeps seeking danger and doesn't know why probably has something it's trying to say.

There's a common misunderstanding that addiction is about pleasure, that addicts are greedy, undisciplined people who don't have any willpower and want every desire indulged without question, like children. But the truth is that once it sets in, addiction is not about feeling good, it's about not feeling terrible. The pleasure found in the hit of one's substance of choice – be that whiskey, nicotine, cocaine, heroin or sugar – is not so much about what it adds, but what it takes away: an immediate curb of anxiety, depression, fear, exhaustion, regret. Boredom. It keeps one's feelings at bay, the great repression. For some, processes work just as well: sex, shopping, gambling, food, lack of food, work, exercise, watching endless hours of television. Behaviours can bring their own highs, but the purpose of the high is not necessarily pleasure in the experience, it's everything the high blots out. One or two custard creams can be a gentle pick-me-up, but the whole packet eaten at once is likely to be doing something else. And when the high wears off, the addict is left depleted, in deficit rather than nourished by pleasure. And hot on the high's heels: shame.

Something as simple as counting my breaths in a room full of strangers, feeling the solidity of the floor beneath my body, made it possible to detect the notes that had been sounding unheard for months.

Stupid girl, said Wormtongue, as a fat tear rolled slowly down my left cheek, and came to rest at the corner of my mouth, a little hint of salt. *Stupid, stupid girl.*

Days later I went to see a man with a machine that would give me many little electric shocks. The physiotherapist was large, the machine was small but very powerful. He attached six electrode pads to the skin on my back and stood beside me as he turned the dial and sent intense pulses of sensation into my shoulder muscles. My body braced against the charge and I thought of the volcano and its subterranean rumbles. I thought of the hysterics at the Salpêtrière and the strange contraptions used to try and cure them. I counted my breathing, one, two, one, two, and felt the weight of the big wet dark city with all its emails and obligations pressing in around me, self-important and empty of meaning. Each time the current filled my body I entered a world of pure sensation where Wormtongue could not follow. It felt like coming up, the way heat rushes up and down the spine, the feeling that your organs are made entirely of jelly. The blue plastic massage table was cool beneath my palms and felt good.

The volcano is not the point. If we go down into the root of the volcano what we find is the lava. The centre of the Earth. The lava is there whether we see it or not, whether the volcano shows it to us or not, whether it erupts or not.

The large man with the electric shock machine asked me, where, exactly, is the source of your pain?

Sunbeam New York

THE SECOND YEAR SOBER

Respect the delicate ecology of your delusions.

– Tony Kushner

INSTEAD OF GOING TO THE source, we went to New York – after a year of descent, Wormtongue insisted we deserved a reprieve. I did not disagree.

We landed to find the city itself was blowing off steam. Vast orange-and-white-striped chimneys interrupted the streets and released clouds of vapour into the air. The roar of traffic dragged me into the present tense: this is what I came for.

Welcome to America, says the man in the AT&T shop as he passes a neat red flip phone from his clammy palm to mine. Pay as you go, with no access to the internet, it fits in my hand like a large, smooth pebble. The air in his shop is artificial, cool when outside the morning sun burns hot. In spite of the air-conditioning, we sweat. I thank him and pay with fake money

– dollars, unnervingly soft, thick with the traces of each hand that's held them.

It's a thrill to think no one yet has my number – I feel unknown and completely new. It's not my city so I'm oblivious to its problems and I move through it protected by the selective vision of the tourist.

Wormtongue doesn't know it yet but I've also come to New York in order to take myself seriously (which is hard because immediately it feels like a dream). In the East Village, on the L train, on the Williamsburg Bridge, I try and try to consider myself real. A real woman, a serious woman, a woman of reality.

Stepping back out into the dense July heat of the Lower East Side, new pebble in my pocket, I wonder if Louise Bourgeois might help me to get real. In 1938 she moved to New York from Paris and lived in the city until her death in 2010. It was the site of her reckonings and her emancipation. She was an artist who transfigured her biggest emotions into things you could see and touch: shame into marble, disgust into bronze. Her practice was a dedicated excavation of the depths of her psyche, but, although she spent years in psychoanalysis, her relationship with it was ambivalent. For Bourgeois, art offered greater respite: 'ART IS A GUARANTY OF SANITY', promises my favourite of her drawings. Its scribbled letters are blocked in with purpose in pencil the colour of sensible lipstick on paper the candy-pink shade of Angel Delight. This piece speaks to me in all tenses, to the little girl whose favourite colour was, in spite of herself, *pink pink pink*, and to the young woman now trying to see her own life as something worth guaranteeing at all.

Every day you have to abandon your past or accept it, and then, if you cannot accept it, you become a sculptor, Bourgeois said.

And then, if you cannot accept it, you become a writer, I thought.

And then, if you cannot accept it, you go to New York.

Louise Bourgeois is the official reason I'm here. Her work is central to my thesis and the combination of her archive at MOMA and the travel grant from my doctoral funding means I can research the material embodiment of hysteria and abandon my past at the same time. (Suspended somewhere between abandonment and acceptance, I chose flight). But before I get to work I have a couple of weeks off to explore the city, and I am electric with excitement.

I'm staying with Kate and Jo at their apartment in the East Village. It's high up and each morning I get dizzy on their tumbling view of skyscrapers slicing up the horizon. I buy a bright red ice lolly in the shape of a rocket and walk the baking streets nearby with slow, deliberate steps. My skin glows with sweat. I pass one man led by five dogs, a pretzel stand, yellow and green cabs, all to the unhinged sound of sirens. Melting ice in my mouth slides down easy as my palms prick with the heat and a guy in a T-shirt with the sleeves rolled up swings out from some scaffolding and gives me a high five, singing, *I just wanna love you baby!*

I'm giddy with all of it, not serious at all, so I catch myself, slow it down and try to act like the grown and sober woman I am here to be. Sober is a tricky word and not one I like. I can't identify with it, though I am it, and have now been for thirteen months and counting. (The shift from counting days to months was a powerful thing that took me seconds to take for granted.) Sober reminds me of frowns and low ceilings, municipal halls. Too close to sombre and colours at the end of the spectrum I rarely want to visit – shades of grey, brown and black.

But I'm not ready to give up on intoxication entirely and New York offers me a different kind of high: it's possible to drink in a city and, in this way, get out of your mind. To be sober but none of its unappealing synonyms – serious, sensible, solemn, severe.

It goes like this: My body's still tuned to the wrong clock but nothing gets me down, not the rats, not the trash, not the blisters on my heels. The city is a lake I wade into. I buy Birkenstocks so I can walk further faster more, Wormtongue is quiet for the first time since my last drink, pavements – *sidewalks* – are thick with hurrying bodies and I'm grateful to lose my face in the mob. I am free of myself, here. *The influential American poet Frank O'Hara lived at 441 East Ninth Street from 1959 to 1963* reads the metallic plaque on the wall at 441 East Ninth Street stuck at eye level between a bar and a sushi shop. *Downtown people and places figure prominently in his buoyant works* it says and I walk on through the stream of souls catching eyes, brushing arms, thinking only of the line, *everything is too comprehensible*, which is Frank's but feels like mine, now. On the corner there's a man with a small dog on his shoulders, it looks like a stuffed toy and it's smiling at me, actually smiling as I pass by so I say hello to its triangular face, Don't mind her, says the human plinth, she's just keeping a lookout. A lookout for what, I think, there are no cats here, until I hit St Marks Place, where in fact historically there have always been cats, although of the jazz variety, and it's all fire escapes and red bricks and Search & Destroy, Gem Spa, Funky Town, Jules Live Jazz, New York's Best Egg Cream. I sit down at a café with a green-striped awning and blue and white mosaic tables, Hello, I say to the waiter, I'll have a black iced Americano please, milk on the side, I say, hamming up my voice so it might cut glass because I am ready to be told I'm cute, that my accent is cute, but the waiter is busy and doesn't notice, just brings the milk in a jug and the tall black coffee. The ice cubes are huge. It's cold in my hand and bitter on my tongue and it does the job and it makes me feel good. Next to me two women who look my age have a conversation I know by heart about their friendship with another, more difficult woman, their astronomical rents, how little envy they feel for the bourgeois luxuries in the lives of the people they know – this one is a lie: cities are a language I speak. I feel the caffeine buzz through me and start tapping my knee even though I have nowhere to be. I'm feeling very optimistic and it's very fucking good, everyone looks sexy and interesting in the midday light and I want to lean over and ask the women, am I sober? Do I seem like a sober woman to you? Sitting here in my red dress that goes see-through in the sun, absolutely high as I've ever been on the rhythms of this place, on its difference, on all its possibility. I'm not wearing a bra, I want to tell them, I've shrugged everything off, I'm here with none of myself and I haven't had a drink for all this time and I'm not even thirsty.

I swallow the now-warm coffee dregs and walk down to Key Food to get out of the heat and I'm floored by the landscape of edible things. Mountains of peaches, mountains of kale, mountains of 'deli salad' all with the same queasy mayonnaise glow. I never knew there were so many kinds of maple syrup: Log Cabin, Aunt Jemima, Vermont Maid, Hungry Jack – original and sugar free, butter rich, low calorie. I buy a Strawberry Snapple and a bottle of water and take a photo of the wall of Paul Newman sauces – *all natural, all profits to charity* – which I post on Instagram to show I've arrived. It's a long walk up to The Met. When I hit the park I'm glad of the green and the shade on my skin and the trees are a watchful rebellion in the high-rise grid. I walk the paths. I'm cocky that I can't get lost but I do get lost and it irritates me and I drink the Snapple and fake pink strawberry flavour floods my senses with the taste of every American trip and I feel OK. The museum is vast and cool and there's so much to see. I walk through galleries of men of action and naked women of mythical beauty thinking, The Guerrilla Girls were right, women do have to be naked to get in here. I imagine being naked in here, and think I'd quite like it. Ancient bodies, soft and rounded bodies like mine made hard and strong by marble, bodies in fragments, beautiful broken bodies. One I get stuck on is the bottom part of a face made of buttercup-yellow jasper, 'Fragment of the Face of a Queen' reads the label that says she's from 1336 BC, which is an impossible time that makes no sense. The little blurb tells me she 'cannot be securely identified' and I think I know how she feels. Her lips are sensuous and full. We are both a long way from home but I'm here by choice. In the café I meet a poet named Vincent who shakes my hand and asks what brings me to the city and I lie and tell him I've moved here forever and he wishes me luck and buys me a pencil from the giftshop. I walk all the way back down to Kate and Jo's and by the time I arrive the city has done its job and I am absolutely spent. I tell them about my day's adventures and Jo laughs and says that Key Food isn't even a good supermarket. Just wait till you see the rest of them, she grins.

That night I dream of having sex and taking heroin and endless fire escapes that lead nowhere.

In the gummy haze of just waking I walk to Washington Square Park to sit on the edge of the fountain and watch the world come to life. A few moments alone with my jet lag in the dawn. Soon I'm joined by a lonely saxophone, and a strange, bearded figure on rollerblades who propels himself along with a walking stick. A boxer arrives and takes off his shirt. Ducking and diving and jabbing, his scarlet gloves are shiny in the sunlight, obscene, like the snapping claws of a lobster. I dare the city to treat me badly, and it doesn't.

I have with me a battered copy of Graham Greene's *The End of the Affair* that I borrowed from a friend back home. It tells the story of a passionate, ill-fated romance, but it's also about the power of guilt and magical thinking. Tucked in between pages eighty and eighty-one is a postcard marking the following passage, where it started to feel as though the book was reading me:

Have I got to give up drinking too? If I eliminate everything, how will I exist? I was somebody who loved Maurice and went with men and enjoyed my drinks. What happens if you drop all the things that make you I?

Here, in her journal the character Sarah Miles is asking herself the question I've been struggling to answer. I've dropped all the same things – love and drinks and 'going with men'. I've eliminated so much that I used to think was part of who I was. A light spray from the fountain grazes my cheek as I try to imagine what other things I might pick up instead. New versions of myself clamour just out of reach. If the old script was: *I was somebody who loved oblivion and went too far and enjoyed getting lost,* what is the new one? *I am somebody who loves walking and goes to the library and enjoys custard creams?*

You've lost your edge, says Wormtongue.

Secretly, shamefully, I agree. What a horror it would be, to be boring.

So when a friend offers to set me up with a guy she knows in the city I don't miss a beat. People have warned me that early recovery involves a cycling through of replacement substances and behaviours – shopping, sugar, coffee, sex – but I feel strong in my resolve. I'm different now. And if I make a mess of it all I'll be leaving when my research trip ends in twelve weeks, each of which already feels like a minute on the march to midnight when I'll abruptly turn into a toad.

Wormtongue says, *Tick tock.*

I descend the stairs from the subway at Knickerbocker Avenue and look out for a brown-haired man in a black T-shirt, which is how Jake described himself in the text he sent. With each step it's a thrill to feel there's no going back. As I near the bottom the body of a man comes into view revealed from the feet up leaning against the black and green metal girder just in front:

black and white converse, black denim skate shorts, black T-shirt, slight side smile, black shades, brown hair.

Jake? I say, as my rubber sole finally hits the pavement on Myrtle.

Over dinner I learn that Jake is a gentle, melancholic artist with guitarist's hands and soft eyes whose intermittent smiles feel like a prize. He smells inexplicably of freshly baked baguettes. For our date he takes me to a fusion restaurant round the corner in Bushwick where we eat Dorito kimchi carbonara and I order a watermelon juice. It comes in a huge jar with a blue cocktail umbrella the same colour as my jumpsuit and I immediately tuck it behind my ear because I am trying to be beguiling.

Fluorescent versions of Pac-Man characters are wall-mounted behind the bar and I feel like I've walked into someone else's trip. The walls are covered in murals of giant sea slugs in neon UV paint that pulse in the blacklight glow, except for one which is a distortion of mirrors. I try not to look at myself and cringe when I catch sight of a monstrous woman, her giant mouth agape in a laugh so wide it's like her jaw is dislocated, and realise with horror that she is me.

Close your big mouth, say Wormtongue and I in unison.

Jake tells me about leaving the Midwest for New York ten years before and I envy him that, the chance to define his own life in a city he can claim for himself. London is heavy with every stage of mine, haunted by the ghosts of younger versions of myself that I'd prefer not to meet, waiting on corners in ambush.

Afterwards we go back to his to watch a film and take our

clothes off in the dark. He tells me the stories behind each of his tattoos, and that he's always had a thing for Brits. Each time before he touches me he asks permission first. It feels good to be a thing that a person might like simply because of an accident of birth.

In the morning we eat pancakes at a diner up the road and the coffee is bad but it doesn't matter because it's diner coffee and that means I'm far from home. When the waitress offers me a refill I say yes please yes that would be lovely yes please, because I really am just so pleased about everything. Cute accent, she says, as she fills up my mug.

But the Lower East Side looks different in the dark and with no map on my phone when night falls I get lost. I'm the daughter of a man who always knows north and can navigate by stars but none of these skills made their way down to me. I text Jake for directions and to my surprise I love feeling like a remote-control girl: left a bit, right a bit, left a bit more, one block up, one block right, turn left, there you are.

Thank you, I'm such a dickhead, I write.

You're not a dickhead, you're just lost! Jake replies.

You are such a dickhead, says Wormtongue. *Who gets lost in a grid?*

Over the next week, Wormtongue gets louder and the thrill of the city starts quietening down. I dream often about drinking and about being drunk, and most days wake up afraid. The heat grows oppressive. Now on the subway a rat is just a rat. The psychiatrist's voice rattles around my brain saying, restless, irritable, discontent to the rhythm of a train and the familiar itch is back in my bones and means I can't be still. But I'm cooked, I think, I'm sober, I'm fixed! Meditation and meetings are things for the sick, recovery is a destination and I've reached it and things should be easy, now. Why aren't things easy now, why don't I feel good?

It's in this frame of mind that I get hooked on the neon signs of psychic shops in the East Village. Their windows heave with gold vases, Egyptian busts, incense and crystals, as if the spoils of The Met have dressed up in drag. Tarot cards fan out on tables under lanterns or kitsch chandeliers. Fluorescent pink or red or yellow cursive letters glow with the promise of pleasure and maybe something illicit, speaking the same language as strip clubs and sex shops and retro-styled bars (I'm trying hard not to notice Manhattan's many bars). Sandwich boards propped up outside offer ten-dollar readings and promises to balance your chakras, cleanse your aura. Abandon your past or accept it. Then seek your future, why not?

Staring at the words *psychic* and *believe* illuminated in bright white neon it hits me that I rarely think about the future at all. Just enough to get the people who care off my back, so I can float through the miasma of time in peace, unencumbered.

Suspended in the present like a beetle in aspic.

The night I meet Kate and Jo for pizza under the Brooklyn Bridge is brooding and humid and matches my mood. We sit in a row facing the water and I look up at the hulking structure as though it were Gulliver and I, a Lilliputian tugging on its ropes.

Hot and greasy in my mouth, the taste of oregano-spiced tomato mixes with the sight of old, heavy steel.

We sit looking back at the night lights of Manhattan and a thick sea mist rolls in. It envelops us totally and eats the skyscrapers opposite one by one: the bridge, the Empire State Building, streetlamp after streetlamp. All gone. We laugh, nervous, and shiver together in the dark as before us, the city blacks out.

Blackouts are not something I believed happened to me when I drank. That's the simple trouble with denial – you don't know it's happening until it slips. And even then, there's no guarantee the knowledge will stick. You might grasp it for a minute or an hour or a day before your psyche does its work and sweeps it back into the shadows. After all, denial is about protection, perverse though it might seem – from pain, from guilt, from too much reality. It buys some time to adjust, a little moment of grace before facing the full force of a change or a loss or a difficult truth. It can be useful, sometimes vital, but trouble hits when you get stuck in this transitional place, glitching between avoidance and recognition.

But alcohol blackouts don't creep up like a majestic fog sweeping in off the East River. They're more like a fire curtain: swift and total coverage. When your blood alcohol concentration reaches a certain point – from above roughly 0.16 per cent, which is twice the legal driving limit – it brings about changes in the brain and impairs the hippocampus, the part that regulates memories and emotional responses. It takes its name from the

Greek for seahorse (*hippokampos* – *hippos* meaning horse, *kampos* meaning sea monster) on account of its shape, like a little curved tube. Though we tend to talk about it in the singular, mammals actually have two hippocampi, one for each side of the brain, and I've come to think of them as watchful guardians, a pair of tiny seahorses keeping things in order in the personality. Once the circuit breaks, so does the capacity to make new memories, and you go from storing an internal temporal imprint of your actions to leaving no trace for yourself at all.

You do, however, leave a trace in the world. You become a body and mind completely untethered. A walking, talking, living doll.

When I drank I'd sometimes wake up with bruises I couldn't account for, hours of lost time. Whole nights pieced together from the memories of others. If this detective work dredged fragmented recollections from the swamp it was creative and fun, shared with friends the morning after over tables heaving with drinks, our hungover thirst irrepressible. We'd build from our combined scraps an *exquisite corpse* of the night before as though we were playing a game of consequences. The times when this collective remembering brought no spark of recognition, brought nothing at all, I'd feel dread in my spine and shrink back from my edges as I listened to my friends tell a story about somebody else, knowing that the subject was me. But in blackout you forget yourself. You drop all the things that make you I.

Looking out across the murky harbour I clung tight to the knowledge that although I couldn't see it, the Empire State Building was still there behind the cloud. Denial is a form of self-hypnosis and I knew that recognising its power was part of recovery. If I could manage to do that, perhaps I'd finally understand that reality was worth holding on to, after all.

The next day I moved into a railroad apartment in Greenpoint, a sublet I'd arranged with a filmmaker named Carlos who I knew through recovery meetings. We'd agreed to swap flats for the summer, both of us craving the familiar alienation of a city that wasn't ours. When we first met over Skype we discovered our matching green living rooms and the twin chaos of images pinned above our desks, which both included the same postcard of Buñuel's *Viridiana* and that picture of Patti Smith from the cover of *Horses* with the black jacket slung over her shoulder. We laughed at the places our lives intersected, our transatlantic echoes, how you're rarely as original as you think you are.

On my way to pick up Carlos's keys I stopped by Canal Street and bought a miniature version of the iconic skyscraper in the form of a keyring. It was metal and 3D, a sharp thing at the bottom of my bag that stabbed my fingers and yanked me back to the real world when later I fished around for the keys in the dark.

As I waited on the subway platform at Union Square in impossible subterranean heat I stared without focus at the scene in front: a grid of steel girders and white ceramic tiles, a Fernet-Branca poster with a hot blonde in a minidress and fishnet tights and the tagline *shockingly unique*. I felt tired and a long way from home.

Things with Jake had grown complicated as I recognised the swelling of a familiar need that wasn't about who he was or what we shared but simply the relief of escaping into the body and mind of someone else. In every quiet moment Wormtongue would whisper, *Text him text him text him has he texted yet text him*, and like an automaton I would feel my fingers moving across the keypad in some combination of letters that strove for nonchalance. If he didn't text back: despair. Either way, Wormtongue would get his fill – both the thrill of acceptance and the ache of rejection are offerings for the void, lines of flight from the present.

On the platform I let my eyes move over the people waiting to go in the other direction and one face in particular gave me a jolt of recognition. My gaze stuck to it as I tried to work out why and how I knew it.

The face belonged to a man in his twenties, like me. His skin was puffy and sallow and one eye was swollen almost entirely shut. He wore a band T-shirt and black jeans, and the slope of his shoulders was desperate. He looked like he hadn't slept in days and moved heavily across the platform. Unnervingly close to the edge, he stopped. I wanted to call out, hey are you OK?! and I also wanted to look away.

More visible now, in the light I saw it wasn't his face I knew but the state of his mind. I understood how it felt to find yourself close to the edge with a train on the way. It was not so long ago that I'd sat in my therapist's office bewildered and scared and confessed that I found my body not my own, even in waking hours when I'd had nothing to drink. That waiting for trains I'd find my feet drawn to the edge as if by magnets and come round to myself standing exactly where a person might if they were planning to jump.

I wanted with all my being to reach the man opposite, put my hand on his shoulder and pull him back from the tracks. At that moment the L train thundered through – a silver bullet – and of course when it had passed he had gone.

At Carlos's place I discovered that Greenpoint, Brooklyn was a good place to wake up. In the mornings before my feelings of dread could settle I'd walk down the avenue towards the East River. At the end of the street was a park with a pier that stretched out towards Lower Manhattan. To the left, an industrial lumber yard and a water tower tagged with pro-Palestinian graffiti. Each day I would walk the length of the pier transfixed by the view, the empty width of 14th Street before me a syncopated beat in the city's climbing rhythm of brick, glass and steel.

I found a reliable way to stifle Wormtongue was to go to the Peter Pan Donut & Pastry Shop and escape his wheedling with a hit of something sweet. Crossing the threshold was like stepping back in time: bright lights, white walls and the caramel scent of melted sugar, waitresses – all women – in teal button-down smocks with baby-pink collars and cuffs, and baby-pink caps embroidered above the visor with *Peter Pan* in thread to match. The menu dedicated a whole section to sweetener: Sugar, Splenda, Sugar In The Raw, Sweet'N Low, Equal, Simple Syrup, Honey. Behind the counter a sign read, 'But First, Coffee', which was kept on the boil and served oily black. Doughnuts climbed the walls laid out in raked trays: glazed and sprinkled and dusted

47

and filled. At the first drop of Wormtongue's poison I would read their names out loud in my head, because a person can find great solace in the predictable rhythm of a list:

Honey Dip, Sugar Raise, Soft Twist, White Cream, Bavarian Cream, Boston Cream, Cream Crumb Old Fashioned, Cream Chocolate Sprinkle, Strawberry Frosted Sprinkle, Honey Dip French Cruller, Plain Jelly, Sugar Jelly, Jelly Stick, Bowtie, Bavarian Éclair, Old Fashioned Volcano With Bavarian Cream, Old Fashioned Volcano With White Cream, Old Fashioned Powder.

They sounded like dance moves and drugs, and brought me some sweet relief.

My days of holiday had come to an end. I threw myself back into my research and after my first morning in the MOMA archives, I went to Peter Pan to quieten my mind. I'd spent hours immersed in fierce air-conditioning and Louise Bourgeois's work: hundreds of images of sculptures and prints and drawings and dolls that tried to make sense of her repressions and anxieties, and the enduring mysteries of the human condition. In her hands we are fragile, yearning, complex creatures, full of longing and joy, revulsion, anger and melancholy. I found solace in her relentless exploration of primal feelings, which I never felt very far from.

Even after I left the gallery, the titles of her pieces swirled around my head like the notes I wrote in my little green book. They spoke in the language of my own fears and longings: *Do Not Abandon Me, She Lost It, Head on Fire, Insomnia, Madeleine, Spiralling Eyes, The Guilty Girl is Fragile, Mr. No Thank You, Umbilical Cord, Femme Maison, Hold My Bones, I Held His Eyes*

Within My Gaze, The Return of the Repressed, Feather Thoughts, Hysterical, I Am Afraid, Turning Inwards, I Lost You, You Are My Polar Star, Headless Woman, I Go To Pieces: My Inner Life, The Endless Loop, Spiral Woman.

Sweets for my sweet, sang Wormtongue. *Sugar for my honey.*

The spiral is a motif that spins through Bourgeois's work across the decades, in prints and sculptures, drawings and fabric pieces. It's a feeling, an action, a state of body and mind. A way of visualising the swirl of anxiety but also the cycle of life, birth and rebirth, time whirling on. It represents control and freedom – the conflicting forces of tightening and unravelling, depending which direction you choose to follow.

In the archive I lost myself to its hypnotic shape, and when I came across a series of drawings called *Spiral Woman* I was surprised to find my eyes fill with tears. The woman is pictured suspended, encased in four bulbous rings of a thick swirl, like a boa constrictor or a stack of tyres. They stretch her head far from the rest of her body, and beneath the rings her belly, arms and legs hang limp. In some, the expression on her face is inscrutable, vacant, and in others the sphere of her head is filled in with the rudimentary markings of a simple smiley face, as if drawn by a child. There's a startling power in recognising your own internal life in someone else's words or images. My body understood before my mind that I knew this state, with all its ambivalence.

Sitting on a high stool at the back of the bakery I let my feet dangle just off the ground. I couldn't stop wondering whether the rings that held the spiral woman were a comfort or a menace – freedom from anxiety or a terrible trap. I decided to escape into full throttle regression. From a stern waitress whose expression fought hard against the candy colours of her uniform I ordered a Red Velvet Volcano. Sweetness is a timeless state. A dessert to desert myself.

I'll never ever let you go.

Bourgeois liked to describe the artist as a figure who never grew up. Peter Pan wasn't an artist but he had things in common with people who build worlds and value play and show us other ways to see – that second sight often shared by artists and children that comes from their desire to get beneath the surface of things, to ask why and how and also why not. Like Peter, they know the value of disobedience, instinct and the immediacy of desire.

I tore off a piece of the volcano and put it in my mouth as I wondered what it really meant to grow up. In a handful of days I'd be twenty-eight, which sounded a long way from childhood to me.

Practically dead, Wormtongue said. *Might as well have fun while you still can.*

In J.M. Barrie's famous stories Wendy is the one who plays at being an adult and eventually does grow up. She betrays her younger self, who wants to stay a child so she can play with Peter forever. The grammar of play isn't so different from the grammar of addiction: a syntax built out of pleasure and denial, fear and fantasy, expressed mostly in the present tense. But at some point for most people life stops being a game and, like Wendy, they do grow up, get real, and accept the complex burdens of a past and a future, where the concept of consequences is able to take shape.

But the thing about Peter Pan is not that he couldn't grow up, it's that he wouldn't.

Sometimes I miss my drunken adventures. Nights spent careening around cities, stumbling across strangers in bars, collecting lost boys and lost girls, lost people bonded together by the thrill of escape – from some mild peril, from our lives, from ourselves. The strange and exciting and often a little frightening places you find yourself at the end of a night when you don't want to go home, watching the sun come up through an unfamiliar window. Drunkenness is a Neverland where you find comrades and enemies, but it's also where you, like Peter, might lose your shadow.

Carl Jung's analytical psychology has its own Peter Pan figure: the *puer aeternus* or *puella aeterna* archetype, the eternal boy or eternal girl. Recognisable in myths, stories, art and dreams, Jung believed archetypes to be hereditary concepts that belong to the collective unconscious and underlie individual experiences. There are archetypal events – like birth, death and separation from parents – and archetypal figures, like the *puella*, or the hero, the father, the trickster, or the sage, as many potential archetypes as situations a person can find themselves in. Sometimes they are balanced out by their opposite – the whimsy and disorder of the *puer/puella* finds its shadow in the *senex*, the wise old man archetype that represents responsibility, rationality, discipline. Though they're at opposite ends of the spectrum, a balanced psyche tempers the playfulness of the *puella* with the gravitas of the *senex*; the wild impulses of the Dionysian with the guiding logic of the Apollonian. Too far in either direction leads to recklessness or calcification, unbounded self-interest or a stultifying solemnity: pleasure-seeking or pleasure-denying and nothing in between.

The aim, of course, is for flexibility – to be able to feel the echoes of all these figures from time to time, but not get stuck in thrall to any of them in particular.

According to Jung, the role of archetypes is to guide us in the process of our self-realisation. He believed that through self-knowledge a person can learn to accept the unconscious parts of their personality, as well as everything presented by the ego. If you manage it, individuation is the reward: a state of integration beyond what he called 'the false wrappings of the persona' and 'the suggestive power of primordial images', or archetypes.

There are plenty you might recognise: the pilgrim and the nurse, the fool and the poet, the gambler, the warrior and the muse, the devouring mother, the temptress, the liberator, the prophet, or the glutton, or the martyr, or the slave. You likely know about the anima, the animus and the shadow. But what about the lost soul, the escapist, the fantasist and the addict? What is the archetype for the compulsive and the recovering? The forgetful drunk, the lost boy, the remote-control girl? The spiral woman?

As I finished the volcano I felt the soft, filmy outline of an ulcer in my mouth. It reminded me of the smooth marble forms of Bourgeois's *Cumul I*, which I'd spent a long time looking at in the archive that morning. The sculpture is a dynamic colony of spheres pushing through the surface of what could be skin or fabric or some other membrane, and, like a mouth ulcer, is both disturbing and compelling. I let my tongue pass over the sore and found another one beside it, felt the complex thrill of the sting, and wondered if they were my punishment for eating too much sugar. I prove to myself time and again that I could never pass the marshmallow test.

I have mixed feelings about Jung's ideas, but in the *puer* and *puella* I recognise myself. Like drunks and small children they struggle with limits. They represent unbounded instinct, disorder and intoxication. They love freedom and independence – restriction of any kind feels intolerable. There are positives to these archetypes: they embody a potential for growth, newness, optimism and excitement. Hope. But they also stand for passivity, self-centredness and a helpless drifting through life. Like Peter Pan himself, a tricky paradox of self-confidence and submission.

And what about the girl who did go and grow up? Breaking the monotonous cycle of addiction was the first step towards a shift in tenses, from the present to something rounded out with past and future too. It was a shifted allegiance from Peter to Wendy, from refusal to responsibility. Her betrayal was one I was starting to see within myself (though I can't deny that there will always be a part of me that's most aligned with Tinkerbell, because, like her, I often only have room for one feeling at a time).

Sweetness spread through me and warmed up my blood. For the moment my one feeling was good.

When I first saw the psychiatrist, the book he recommended was called *The Addictive Personality: Understanding the Addictive Process and Compulsive Behaviour*, by psychologist Craig Nakken. He asked me to read it, with the caveat that it was published in the '80s so the language was often old-fashioned. It's a short book with the kind of dated cover that identifies its home as the self-help section at the library – muddy, clashing colours overlaid with a bewildering mixture of different fonts.

Like the dutiful student I was trained to be, I began my reading on the bus home, hiding the book's cover against the bag on my knees out of a shame which I was unsure whether to put down to embarrassment at my dysfunction or literary snobbery. Probably it was both.

I read about the process of addiction and its different types of high – the intense, raw power of Arousal, the feeling of completeness and comfort from Satiation, and the reassuring detachment of Trance. I read that addicts seek to feel excited, relaxed or in control, and eventually turn to objects or processes to meet those needs over the complication and unreliability of other human beings. I read about their pathological desire to get through life with the least pain and most pleasure possible, and recognised myself. The archetypal addict – pleasure seeker, reality dodger, escapist, avoidant, lost.

As long as an addict's illness is active, argues Nakken, they remain trapped in an eternal adolescence. When I reached Part 3, titled 'The Why of Recovery', I tossed the book aside, thinking, I don't need this, I'm not a junkie, the psychiatrist is being so *dramatic*.

But now 'The Why of Recovery' was where I lived and it was these different kinds of high that came to mind as I sat at the counter eating the volcano and thinking of Peter Pan. Increasingly I was beset by the swell of cravings for any and all things. I wanted sugar sugar sugar all the time, sugar and sex and coffee and things, anything to offer the insatiable void. It was like the first two weeks of bliss had been a movie and now people had come to dismantle the set: my new city high was gone and in its place was restless frustration. I was in mourning for the story of my balanced new life. I wanted to stay in that ideal place where everything went my way and nothing felt hard, but now I was having to face the fact that the fantasy of a recovery worked for and obtained and *finished* was falling apart.

I paid the bill and walked home, my skin crawling with angst. Writing up my notes from the archives back at the flat, the screen of my laptop multiplied in my vision. More ulcers continued to bloom on my gums and I became fixated that somehow I'd consumed the sculpture *Cumul I* and my mouth would soon turn to marble.

By the evening I had a fever and no idea where I was.

The next day passed in delirium and dreams. When finally I awoke my mouth was ablaze with ulcers and everything hurt. Aching and dazed, I somehow managed to get a taxi to the hospital, where they asked about insurance first. In my wallet were the details of the policy my father had made me take out, something I'd never have got around to myself. As I clutched the small plastic card in my hand I felt a deep swell of gratitude for his foresight.

A nurse sat me in a wheelchair behind a curtain in the busy ER and took syringes of my blood, an impossibly vivid red. A doctor in green scrubs arrived and worried about the ulcers, which were angry and sore, and meant I had struggled to eat. Did I use intravenous drugs? he asked, very serious. Could I have HIV?

When the test came back negative the doctor – a young man in thick spectacles who looked like Buddy Holly – said, You're going to be OK but I'm afraid you have Coxsackievirus. I laughed and made a joke about not sucking many cocks and he said, Ma'am, and looked me dead in the eye, unsmiling, Coxsackievirus is not a sexually transmitted disease. I did my best to look equally serious and waited as he wrote a prescription for a pink morphine mouthwash that tasted like chalk and old mints. He told me to eat ice cream until the ulcers receded and sweat it out at home.

Because I was contagious nobody could visit. Everything broke down. I had groceries delivered but my mouth was too tender to eat. Hunger-addled hours were spent with the bedroom door shut against the heat which came through from the kitchen where the air-conditioning didn't reach. In the company of delusions I sucked on cubes of ice and slipped between tenses in the evening half-light.

I am visited by the yellow queen with the fragmented face but now she has a body too, muscular and strong and soft like rubber. Do not abandon me, she whispers. Let's go to the old-fashioned volcano. It's not far, just follow me, second star to the right and straight on till morning. She leads me to a beach of grey sand where we meet a man with my name embroidered on his back pocket. As he stands up he grows to double his height and I see he has a thick moustache and small wire spectacles and I understand that he is a philosopher. He takes me by the hand and says, *We have all hidden gardens and plantations in us; and by another simile, we are all growing volcanoes, which will have their hours of eruption: how near or how distant this is, nobody of course knows.* I know you, I tell him, you've told me that before. Yes, he smiles, you read it in one of my books, *The Gay Science*, my name is Friedrich and I'm here to take you to the spiral woman. She's gone to pieces but we can put her back together with sugar jelly if you like. The words Wise Old Man glow above his head in neon and follow him wherever he goes. My hand is tiny in his. Clutched to my chest in my other arm is a small baby with wisps of fair hair. I am rotting, it informs me calmly, you need to change me I am rotting. I'm sorry, I tell it, I'm sorry I try to say again but there are too many words like chunks of biscuit in my mouth and crumbs are tumbling everywhere so I lie down just for a minute in the powdery snow, except it's not snow it's icing sugar and I sink beneath it and I cease to breathe.

On the fifth day my fever broke. On the sixth, I came out of my delirium for long enough to eat some soup and check my email, where I found a message from my father:

How are things in New York? Sweltering I expect.
Never mind – golf gets worse and the news is awful but
it will all change soon – nothing stands still for long.
  Hope you are enjoying yourself. America has the most

good, the most bad and the most banal of any country I know; you just have to be choosy.

Lots of love.

Dad

I wanted to reply, I've fallen out of time and I don't know where I am. I swallowed a sculpture and my mouth makes no sense. Please come and get me. Instead I wrote that New York was great, hectic and mad but that I was enjoying every minute, that I had to go but I promised to write properly later.

The truth was we were both concealing something – the eternal girl and the wise old man. You wouldn't know it from his email but I'd soon discover that he too was beginning to slip somewhere out of time.

When finally I was well enough to face the day with clean hair I scrubbed Carlos's flat from top to bottom as though the virus might still be lurking behind the curtains or under the bed. In the kitchen I found the bin was full of maggots. It had baked unemptied in the heat for the duration of my fever. The ulcers were almost all gone and it felt as though they had slipped from my body and transmuted into the teeming mass before me. Decay is never far away, I thought, remembering the poor squirrel that died in my attic back home.

Still gathering my strength, in one day I watched all six episodes of Jane Campion's *Top of the Lake*. Set in a remote New Zealand town it tells the story of a lost girl and the woman detective (played by Elizabeth Moss) who tries to find her. In it there is a guru called GJ played by Holly Hunter, who runs a women's camp at the water's edge built out of shipping containers strung with lights. Sitting stately in a low chair with long grey hair falling over her shoulders she speaks with gravelly intensity to Elizabeth Moss, but her words came out of the laptop and landed as though she were speaking directly to me: *So, you are on your knees? Good. Now die to yourself. To your idea of yourself. Everything you think you are, you are not. What's left? Find out.*

Find out.

From my sickbed I returned to the world recovered and hungry. The hunger was fierce and specific: it wanted to consume food and it wanted to consume art, which is to say, it was a hunger to be transported. I was still shaken by the wilderness of my night-time visitations and was determined to take seriously the messages they delivered. Afraid I might open my jaw so wide as to eat the whole city I first took myself to a meeting.

The meeting in Brooklyn was reliably similar to the London ones I'd grown used to: the same giveaway of a cluster of people smoking outside an unassuming doorway, and inside, the same scrolls and slogans pinned up on the walls: *Keep Coming Back. It Works If You Work It. Easy Does It. One Day At A Time.* At first these phrases had seemed like lame platitudes or cultish mantras, but now I welcomed their simplicity.

As the meeting got started I glanced down to switch off my phone, and when I looked back up sitting opposite me was the man from the subway with the beat-up face who had appeared so derelict a couple of weeks before. His face was still bloated and bruised, but he sat with his shoulders back and his head up and seemed much better. He shared that he was under ninety days sober and I realised that the day I'd seen him was likely the tail end of his last bender. The addict in me recognises the addict in you, I thought.

As usual, once the chatter of Wormtongue's resistance quietened down, it soothed my mind to hear my condition described in the mouths of strangers who shared it. My hunger was their hunger, and their hunger was mine. We confessed our loneliness, frustration and fear, our longing for a drink or a line or a fuck or a smoke or a pill or a bet or a hit of whatever the void called for that day. It didn't matter in whose voice the words were spoken, in essence it felt like they belonged to all of us.

What I also found was a truth I'd been skirting ever since my first meeting: that recovery is a process a person can't rush. That just as you spiral down, you spiral up – there are peaks and troughs, no linear path, you just have to keep putting one foot in front of the other.

I spent my last weeks in New York in the archives and visiting every gallery and museum I could think of. My twenty-eighth birthday fell right at the end of the trip. To celebrate, Kate and Jo took me to Coney Island, where we ate hot dogs on the pier and put our feet in the sea. Candyfloss and neon lights and people strutting up and down the boardwalk, all sunkissed elbows and knees. *The pennycandystore beyond the El / is where I first / fell in love / with unreality*, recited Lawrence Ferlinghetti in my mind, his voice expressive, musical. *Jellybeans glowed in the semigloom*, he told me, as the sun began to slide down towards dusk. I sank into the thrill of speed on the rollercoaster as we spiralled up, spiralled down. At the sideshow we watched a woman breathe fire and a man swallow a sword and a person charm a snake and secretly I imagined another life where I let myself keep unravelling, where I didn't try to recover at all.

Back in London I struggled against the beat of my own city. It was all too known and offered me nothing but the real. I tried smothering it with a tracing of New York, moving through familiar streets trying to see them as if for the first time, to feel myself new in them, seeking out the city's busiest corners where I might get high on the crowd, but it never worked. Each face seemed like one I already knew. Restless, irritable, discontent.

I had work to do but I didn't want to be where I was and meeting a stranger can be like visiting a new place, so at Wormtongue's insistence I invited over a man I'd been talking to online.

His was one of several names that would appear as notifications on the screen of my phone and offer a momentary thrill, the pull of the unknown. With the flick of a finger I could call up a catalogue of faces to either save or discard, each entry in the app like a Top Trumps card around which my imagination could build a story: *Man With Puppy, Man With Bun, Man With Women, Man With Muscles, Man With Mountain, Bald Man, Scuba Man, Man With Sideburns, Man Wearing A Wide-brimmed Hat.* Each one a potential trap door out of the present. Plenty about it felt cheap and callous − like a marketplace for sex and love that reduced its members to caricatures, me included – but for a while it was a good distraction and I didn't think too hard about what I was using it for.

This man was good company, with confident hands and sharp canine teeth that caught the light when he smiled. He was tall, his long body solid and unfamiliar, his fingers heavy with silver rings. That night in my bed he stroked my skin and told me stories of Paros, of lambs to the slaughter and octopus fishing. You stab them, he said, propping himself up on one arm and jabbing at me with the other to demonstrate. Then you reach around the back of their heads to pull off the ink sac, take them by their tentacles and – this bit's a little brutal – bash them repeatedly against a rock. Pulverising the meat, he said with a grin. Again and again and again against the rock. Then you turn the head inside out and scrub it madly with the saltwater until it all froths up. Then you pan fry.

I can't eat octopus, I told him. I feel an affinity with them, because of my name. Or maybe it's your eight legs, he said, flashing those teeth. I liked listening to him talk but I was impatient to disappear into sex, into pleasure. I wanted to get out of my head.

Instead, as we kissed, I found myself entirely absent from my body. While the wolfish man tried to find what pleased me I became completely untethered, unable to feel the weight of his touch. I watched the scene from the doorway as his hands and mouth moved here and then there and the woman on the bed in front of me went through the motions of a fulfilling encounter, but my body was not my own.

The fault wasn't his. I wanted both the sex and the company but I felt no pleasure, no closeness, just empty and numb, as if some vital channel had closed off completely. The unfillable void had opened up, like when you drink and drink and drink but can't seem to get drunk.

It used to work. The first time I asked a stranger to come over I was only a few months sober and the thrill in itself was its own kind of high. At an AA meeting I heard someone say it was best to avoid sex in early recovery when you're vulnerable and raw without your usual fix. This wasn't something I wanted to hear so I left the meeting early and invited round a man from the app who I'd been texting – he made me laugh and I liked the look of his ironic moustache.

Determined to have an adventure, I put a Grace Jones record on and dressed myself in a sheer dress and a golden necklace made of skulls. When I answered the door we kissed and he offered me a bottle of wine. For an instant I was tempted, but told him I was sober so he drank it all himself. The encounter was fun and transporting, which is what I'd hoped for, though I can see now the sex was the least important part. What I was into was the risk.

But this time, with the wolfish man, I got none of what I wanted – not the thrill, not the pleasure – and it left me feeling worse. He left when morning came and I was glad of the daylight and to be alone. When coffee boiled in the Moka on the stove I was comforted by its rich smell, proof that I did still live inside my skin, but loneliness soon came on, like nausea.

You are impossible to please, Wormtongue said.

I ignored him and posted a picture of myself on Instagram, traces of the hot sun of a New York summer still faintly visible on my face though it was autumn now. I hoped those little red hearts might blunt the feeling of loss. Scrolling the faces and places and things on my feed I felt the paradox of these strange virtual forums – there we all were, displaying idealised versions of ourselves in perky little squares, boldly demanding admiration, desire, maybe even love. But pulsing up against that fragile veneer were all our deepest vulnerabilities – our vanity, our loneliness, our longing – caught somewhere between concealment and exposure. Then someone liked my picture and I simply felt good.

Beside my makeshift altar, the book about the addictive personality lay open on the floor. Picking it up to put it away I saw the words PAY ATTENTION in my own handwriting written in the margin next to a vigorously underlined sentence: *Recovery is the continued acceptance of addiction and the continuous monitoring of the addictive personality in whatever form it may take.*

I didn't remember reading it at all.

Sounds like a load of old nonsense to me, said Wormtongue.

The Housewoman

THE THIRD YEAR SOBER

Sometimes I long to forget . . . It is painful to be
conscious of two worlds. – Eva Hoffman

IF ADDICTION IS ROOTED IN the will to forget, recovery is
an act of remembering – a slow reconnection with the parts
of yourself that slipped out of reach while you hungered for
escape. While I was trying to rebuild myself, it became clear my
father was sliding in the opposite direction. The edifice of his
mind had begun to dismantle itself brick by brick. For some
time forgetfulness had been growing in him, slow as lichen – my
mother and I knew it and did not want to know it so we became
forgetful too, complicit in the cover-up of a truth too terrible
to mention. I've since thought that one of the most complex
dynamics in a family is navigating everyone's right to denial.

Although it was reasonable for a man in his early eighties to
lose track of certain things (keys, glasses, telephone numbers), by

the summer of 2015 I noticed a different tenor to these losses. It was not just objects that fell out of his mental net but occasionally now facts and basic skills too.

The first time he forgot how to drive we were in rush-hour traffic on a busy London road, bathed in the warmth of a low evening sun. Through my open window the city smelled of hot tarmac and petrol. With a nervous laugh he took his hands off the wheel in wonder, looked at me and said, I have no idea what I'm doing. Thinking it a joke I laughed too – it was how I felt most of the time. But when I saw the smile on his face was one of uncertainty, not mischief, a prickle of fear danced its way up the back of my neck. I didn't know how to drive, and we were in the middle of three lanes of cars.

Well, that thing's the wheel which you use to steer, I said, pointing at it, with one eye on the red light up ahead. That's the accelerator and that, there, is the brake. The light clicked to amber. I prepared to hit the hazard button while frantically wondering what else I could do.

A real adult would have got their licence by now, Wormtongue said. *But you've always been so lazy.*

Fuck OFF, I whispered.

What? said my father.

The light went green and as quickly as he'd forgotten, my father seemed to remember himself. On autopilot he changed gear and inched forward with the other cars as though nothing had happened, then drove me the rest of the way home as normal. It felt as though I held my breath until we pulled up outside my flat. What happened back there? I asked with more frustration in my voice than I'd intended, but he had no idea what I was talking about.

After that my father started regularly to get lost. For a man who had lived in the city longer than I'd been alive, and whose sense of direction was usually unbeatable, this took some getting used to. For me, the child who believed he would always be my compass, it seemed as though the world had started to spin in the wrong direction.

I needed to pin myself to a moment in space and time so once again I went to lie on a massage table in front of a man with an electric machine. This time, instead of delivering therapeutic shocks, it powered a needle charged with ink that would puncture my skin hundreds of times, leaving indelible traces behind. The man was an artist and the machine was his tool, my body the page he would draw on.

It's funny what we tell ourselves to make sense of complicated things. It was true that I liked tattoos and simply wanted to adorn my skin. But it was also true that I was there to avoid pain in the mind by submitting to it in the body – I knew that it would work, and in the face of whatever chaos was brewing in my father's mind, it made me feel like there was something I could control. *Grant me the serenity*, so the famous prayer goes, *to accept the things I cannot change, courage to change the things I can, and wisdom to know the difference.*

It was not the first time this artist had inked my skin. Between the end of my first love and the end of my drinking I visited his studio with the intention of taking my body back for myself. After being lost to love I wanted to be found in the autonomous thrill of permanently changing my appearance. The sensation as his needle juddered against my ribcage while he did his work gave me the feeling of a line I could cross, an action to cut through the fog of overwhelming emotions. The intensity was thrilling. As soon as he finished I thought about when I would come back.

This time once again music filled the studio and I handed my nerves over to its immersive sound – languid piano layered over a rolling drumbeat which merged to make the impression of a welcome storm. On my torso was a stencil of the design the artist had made me. He called his style 'sacred geometry', and the intricate pattern he'd drawn followed the line of my sternum from between my breasts all the way down to my belly button.

You have good proportions for this design, he said, his French accent strongest on the vowels. Very symmetrical. Under the bright, angled light I revelled in his approval. Rectangles of masking tape covered my nipples and I imagined myself through his eyes as a series of shapes that fitted together well, circles and triangles and squares arranged to make the form of a woman. The stencil was an electric blue though the ink itself would be black. I stared down the length of it, propped up on my elbows. It would take several hours to complete the design and I was eager for the sensation to carry me away.

Thinking about it now it seems strange that I got a tattoo to avoid thinking about my father – he was of a generation that thought them crass and when I was younger he told me explicitly not to get one. But, like many only children I have known,

I've spent my life struggling against enmeshment with my parents, caught in the tension of wanting to please them because I love them and wanting to rebel against them because I want to live for myself.

In the studio the music's beat intensified. The artist turned up the volume and I felt it in my guts, steady and strong. Ready? he asked, and pulled on a pair of black latex gloves, serious and controlled as a surgeon. Ready, I answered, and lay flat on my back. What's this song called? I wanted to listen again later, and use it to return to this place in my mind. Time Is the Enemy, he told me. I prepared myself for the pressure and the sting and wondered if it was true.

Pain can be a powerful call to presence, or it can send you reeling. This time it worked as I'd wanted and I found myself united in body and mind, held by the confines of a single intention. The needles buzzed and whined, and the quality of their sound changed when they chattered against my breastbone. Wormtongue was silent and the creeping dread I had lately been unable to shake eased with each hit. I was high on the thrill of it. Just as he taught me, the artist and I fell into a concentrated rhythm of steady, mirrored breaths. On his inhale and my exhale he pressed down hard onto my sternum, like a resuscitation. There was nothing to remember and there was nothing to forget: the rest of the world fell clean away. I got exactly what I came for.

It didn't take long for the feeling to wear off and put me right back where I started, squaring up to some shapeless dread. Within weeks my mother and I found our denial was finally undone by a plate of her mushroom linguine. Radio 4 was playing in the background as the three of us sat around the table in the kitchen where my parents had first taught me how to eat. A vase of yellow tulips glowed in the warm lamplight and though it was a mild night my father huddled against the radiator for warmth. I felt the fresh ink beneath my T-shirt like a secret.

I can't remember what to do, my father said for the second time. He held his empty fork before him as though it were an alien object and we all looked at it in confusion. What do I do, he asked, a tremble creeping into his voice, with this? My mother's fork was hidden in an elegant twist of pasta which she had twirled up from her plate against the curve of her spoon, and he looked from it to his own redundant utensil in agitated bemusement. I followed his gaze, and understood. The silver metal of my father's empty fork suddenly seemed charged with an electric current, so significant was its meaning, and for a moment we all froze, lost, caught in a tableau: the mother, the escapist and the wise old man.

Sometimes it only takes a small tremor to bring down a big wall. In the kitchen in the lamplight fear changed the shape of my father's eyes as he realised a fork is not something it's normal to forget how to use. There was no more pretending. Adrenaline shot through me and brought me back inside my skin. We, my mother and I, now in some vital way forever separated from him by the fullness of our cognition, reached for laughter like cats chasing a ribbon. We wanted to wrap him in humour and solutions. We wanted to make it all right. She cut up his pasta while I showed him another way to load the fork up with mushrooms and the relief on his face was so childlike I wanted to scream.

Late that summer a wildflower meadow grew on London Fields, and I could not stop looking in the mirror. My face was changing, and not just with age. Within the architecture of my bones I was letting something go.

After the night with the linguine I withdrew into myself. My fears about the bomb that was clearly ticking inside my father's brain made me feel itchy for escape, and by this point sobriety had lost its newness and with that any hint of glamour. I was scared of having a relapse. Walking past pubs overflowing with flushed, happy drinkers I tried to sell abstinence to myself as a radical choice but it was lonely up on my high horse – I'd rather be down in the throng below. It wasn't so much that I craved the taste of alcohol. It didn't register in the body as an impulse or desire for the substance itself, it was a seed that grew instead in my mind, where almost without my noticing, I was starting to romanticise what drinking could offer me. It came in semi-conscious daydreams, a rose-tinted picture of relaxation and conviviality, like those adverts for strong liquor you sometimes see at the cinema, where a beautiful group of friends have a golden good time, and no one ends up in tears or in a fight or in hospital. A vision of what drinking in moderation must be like. What it had been like, when I had been able to do it. And the further I was from the chaos of where things had ended up, the easier it was to forget the truth. My sobriety was beginning to feel both mundane and fragile and I understood I'd need to work harder to protect it.

And so every Sunday morning I would walk beneath the plane trees, proud in their orderly rows, until I reached the meadow. It covered an area the size of a football pitch, and first appeared the summer of my accident in Milan. Then, I had stood on my grazed legs watching butterflies and bumblebees feasting on nectar, transfixed by the electric blue of the cornflowers.

Before its arrival, by high summer the fields were always a wasteland of grass flattened by crowds and baked brown in the sun. The scorched marks of disposable barbeques would make patterns on the ground, and the sun would come up over discarded cans of Red Stripe and overflowing bins as I made my way home from wherever my friends and I had seen off the night. One bright day, there it was, and I wanted to fall in line with its cyclical blossoming.

I would go early to spend time alone with the poppies and the cow parsley, the daisies, pink and white cosmos, and other things I didn't know the names of. The grasses came up almost to your shoulder if you sat down among them, and there it was easy to think about difficult things – they could flutter at the corner of your vision in the lightly honey-scented air and you could choose to look at them or simply turn away.

The meadow wasn't the only reason I was to be found in London Fields at 8 a.m. on a Sunday. The meeting where I had become a regular happened on the other side of the park from where I lived, and we, the recovering, would gather outside to drink coffee and smoke cigarettes before getting down to the business of remembering ourselves. Each time we would listen to the stories shared by other addicts and we would hear ourselves in their words so we didn't forget the truth of our affliction, a disease with the power to forget itself again and again and again.

Wormtongue hated it – every week he'd try to talk me out of going.

It was at this meeting that I met a man whose response to me had long been a heady mix of attraction and indifference. He had been in recovery for several years but I vibrated with the raw, hungry energy of the newly sober and grasped at thrills wherever I could find them – a blossoming crush seemed a safe enough option. We flirted with a connection intermittently but it never went anywhere real. Still, the embers it left behind were enough to fuel a desire that was more than anything an exercise of imagination, with just enough relation to the real to keep the fire stoked but all the freedom of a play script where I could write both parts.

As my father's forgetfulness slowly eroded more of his mind I transferred my longing for his coherence onto my longing for this man. It felt easier, somehow, for the pain to be about unrequited desire instead of the invisible and unstoppable force that was stealing someone I loved away.

How very Freudian, Wormtongue said. *I didn't think you were so basic.*

Neither did I, I wanted to scream, as I teetered between mourning and melancholia. But if you're someone who feels a need to get out of your head it's easy to find yourself in thrall to longing. At its heart, longing is something to do. It can fill the gap left by something you're trying to forget, or the opening made by something you want but are afraid of – longing enlivens time while you hold yourself in stasis, in the dark space between knowing and not-knowing, between action and inaction.

The point of my crush was the fantasy of a love story of which I could be the sole author: it had more to do with the avoidance of love than with love itself. After my experience with the wolfish man I had become wary of my body – its desires felt untrustworthy, like cravings in disguise. I knew I needed to take some time to figure these things out but I feared the emptiness of celibacy and losing the pleasure of a romantic thrill, so I climbed up into the attic of my brain and let the safety of an unfulfilled wish protect me. On my visits to the meadow in 2015, as I sat among the flowers I wanted to know how to stop myself from turning pleasures into poisons.

That was also the year I spent a lot of time looking at a poster for Pedro Almodóvar's film *The Skin I Live In*, which I was writing a chapter of my thesis about. Designed by Juan Gatti, it shows a skinless person standing framed by wildflowers, their muscular body pictured from behind in an extraordinary lattice of sinew and bone. Next to the person, a pink flamingo investigates the mound of grass on which they both stand, and a giant passionflower winds its vine above their heads. (There were passionflowers that grew in the streets near my flat and their pale petals and bright blue coronas always reminded me of the caper flowers on Stromboli. I felt the echo of the volcano when I passed them.)

I knew something of what it was like to feel skinless, but never to feel skinless and strong. Here was a person who had shed their skin on purpose so we might appreciate the intricate anatomy beneath. Their exposed muscles were thick and developed, full of power. It was as though in losing their skin they had been returned to an essential state of truth – the simple potential of a functioning organism: beautiful, complex, natural. Out in the open.

The last six months of my drinking life had felt like a constant shedding. A backward slide, the dissolution of boundaries that were fragile to begin with. I could no longer contain myself and by then I had ceased to try. Though over two years now stretched between me and that version of myself, I could still be made breathless by the memory of my vulnerability then, and the shame of it. Mostly I tried to forget it. I had left parts of myself around the continent like crumbs, often with other people, some of whom were tender with them and some of whom were not. The spiral of my personhood had unravelled and in the years since, I'd worked hard to remake it.

You already know I've been skinless in the literal sense, but I haven't yet told you the whole of that story. What I didn't tell you is that after we came off the bike in the rain and the road claimed a layer of my body for its own, the man with the white Yamaha and I did not immediately go to hospital. Not long after our fall a car had taken the same turning and picked out our bodies on the tarmac in the beam of its lights. The driver, a man who smelled of cigarettes and wine, helped us up and put me in his front seat, balanced on my good hip. He drove me to an all-night pharmacy and the man with the white Yamaha followed on his scraped but still working machine behind.

My memory here is hazy but I know that it hurt too much to stand. A woman in rectangular glasses came out to take a look and spoke to the men in quick-fire Italian. There was a paper bag full of dressings and pills. The words *ospedale, domani* and *polizia*. The man with the car then followed the man with the white Yamaha who led the way back to his flat, where both men helped me up the stairs. I swallowed some pills for the pain. They were strong. The man with the car left and the smell of wine left with him. The man with the white Yamaha and I drank something bracing and he took off his leathers and I took off my wet and blood-stained dress because it stuck painfully against my wounds. I was filled with the thrill of survival and the rush of adrenaline and I wanted to be free of all constraints. All that existed was now.

We sprayed my raw skin with the iodine sold to us by the pharmacist and the sting of it took me to the edge of myself and I laughed until tears streamed down my face and we kissed like a couple of outlaws.

The pills kicked in and the pain subsided. The adrenaline worked to mask my fear and I decided my wounds were just a graze. My blood was everywhere and we chose not to see it. We played loud music and we smoked cigarettes. We had survived something and so we had sex. I remember standing naked on his bed with a whiskey in my hand swaying to the sound of guitars and feeling like I'd got away with it. Just a graze, I told myself. A big graze. I felt wild, essential somehow. Powerful. As if I had crossed a line and perhaps this was where I would stay, here in this place where nothing mattered.

Eventually I fell asleep until I was woken in the dark by the steady build of a terrible pain. A prickly heat stung up the back of my right leg from my ankle to my thigh with growing intensity. There was a deep pulse in my foot. My elbow and shoulder ached, and my knees, and my head. I tried to move from lying on my stomach to reach the pills that were on the floor but the pain was too bad, like my skin was on fire. I heard a murmuring sound to my left and opened my eyes to find the man with the white Yamaha kneeling by the side of the bed, his forehead against my hand, whispering, *Mi dispiace, mi dispiace, perdonami, mi dispiace.*

It made me feel like a statue of someone holy in a church from whom he was seeking forgiveness. I put my hand on his head like a blessing. Hey, it's OK, it's not your fault. The pills? *Pillole?* Can you get me the pills? I pulled myself up onto my good side as my eyes adjusted to the gloom. My leg was a mess of wet red and orange. With gritted teeth I bent my knee to have a look at the throb in my foot and saw there was a small but deep gash down to the bone. The smell of cigarettes and sex and stale alcohol filled the room. The man with the white Yamaha stood and opened the curtains enough to let in a little of the dawn glow and I saw myself clearly for the first time: an accident victim in a stranger's blood and iodine-streaked sheets a long way from home.

Though the things that happen to us may be fixed points in the past, the meaning they carry changes over time, as we learn more about ourselves and our motivations, and as they get distorted by memory or reshaped by perspective. This is a story I've told for laughs, and to shock, and to make myself sound exciting. There's a longer version and a shorter one, a gorier one and a sexier one. It was only once I was into my third year of recovery that I could see it straight and started to be able to tell it like it was: the actions of a person who didn't care about their future at all.

Sometimes the urge to tell everything is about catharsis, sometimes it's bravado, sometimes both, but exhibitionism is not the same as intimacy – one is surface where the other is depth. I hesitated to include that story here, where it might become a commodity, a silver coin in the confessional economy that thrives on tales of feminine dysfunction. But maybe the most important lesson I learned in that meeting across the meadow was the power of telling the unvarnished truth about the places addiction can take you. It takes time to let go of the glamorising, or the minimising, or the exaggeration of a story that fills you with shame – what stung the most was recognising the potential toll of my recklessness, the worse fates narrowly avoided. Without a storyteller's spin, the bare facts are far more exposing. But when you do let go, that's when your vulnerability can become strength – when you can truly be both skinless and strong.

I'm reminded of a quote from the artist Marlene Dumas, whose intimate and unsettling work I admire: *At the moment my art is situated between the pornographic tendency to reveal everything and the erotic inclination to hide what it's all about.* Her often explicit paintings of women explore the tension between display and concealment, between nakedness and nudity, what it really means to 'bare all'. For women and anyone with a marginalised identity in particular, vulnerability exists in a trap – our society is hungry for it, and often expects and demands it as the barrier for entry in order for us to be a subject worthy of attention. We are culturally primed for this kind of pay-off. I wonder how it's made you feel, reading this passage, whether you feel closer to this authorial voice now or more distanced from it?

These are the simple facts, or as close as I can get to them given the state I was in at the time. Maybe they are shocking, but the truth of it is that they were never that shocking to me. In fact, when the bike began to skid and I felt my body start to fall I was flooded with a resignation that struck me then as real liberty. Of course this is how it ends, I thought. I even remember smiling.

In the years since, I have been haunted by the idea that I made it happen, that I opened my arms with a laugh and chose chaos. It isn't true. Though of course on some level it is: to get on a motorbike with drink flooding your blood is a decision to follow the call of the void, the question is only, will you and anyone who crosses your path survive it? When I found myself back under the needle for the second time I can see now that what I wanted was a controlled path back to the limitless place I'd found on the other side of safety, that feeling of freedom I discovered in risk. And in the intensity of pure enveloping sensation, of pain, even, I did find it. But I also knew that it was not the solution it promised to be – it was not a place I could stay forever.

In Gatti's poster, at the feet of the skinless figure lies a chrysalis. Beside them, a fat caterpillar climbs a stem and colourful butterflies and moths dart between the flowers, more majestic than the cabbage whites that kept me company in the meadow that summer, but emblems of metamorphosis all the same. In the aftermath of feeling out of control it's hard to see the mess one makes as anything other than destructive. But if I hold the tender image of that wild, injured girl next to Gatti's illustration of evolution and growth I can see it all differently, as an essential stage in the process of becoming something else. Chaos is generative, after all.

As the days grew shorter and the leaves started to turn, when I looked in the mirror I saw a body marked with ink at its moments of transition and I understood that something had been set in motion. What I saw was a woman letting go of a lost girl, and a lost girl clinging on in fury. I felt the logic of the chrysalis pulse through me, and knew it was time to retreat.

In the 1940s Louise Bourgeois made a series of paintings and drawings all called *Femme Maison*, female nudes whose heads or upper torsos are encased by houses, with their lower bodies left naked and exposed underneath. The title, which literally means 'woman house' or 'house woman', is a play on 'housewife' – when she made them, Bourgeois was raising her three children and exploring the tension between the house as a symbol of refuge and also a prison.

In these images I saw how the things we seek refuge in – identities or relationships, substances or even beliefs – can easily become traps that work against our emancipation. I found their vulnerability moving and felt a deep affinity with the women and their ambiguous symbolism: are they naïve or knowing, are they trapped or protected by the structures that enclose them?

With the tools I was learning at the meetings I attended I worked to build this new refuge called Recovery and tried my best to monitor and accept my addictive tendencies whenever they showed up. But as I turned further away from the mess and risk and pleasure of living I often wondered whether this new structure was nurturing or simply restrictive in a different way – if in moving from the house of addiction to the house of recovery I was still nowhere closer to actually being free. I still felt just as exposed as the house women with their soft, naked bellies and legs vulnerable to the elements. More vulnerable than I had felt before I got sober because I could no longer lean on my fix. The powerful difference between feeling vulnerable and actually being vulnerable hadn't yet sunk in.

The *femme* I liked the best was a line drawing of a woman whose top half is a multi-storeyed building with arches in the basement and an asymmetric smattering of windows over three floors. On either side of the door are two semi-circles that give the house a suggestion of downcast eyes, and one small arm hangs down from the foundations while another, even tinier, waves from the other side. Her body extends beneath in gentle curves, and her feet turn slightly outwards, as if she studied ballet as a child. She stands there, desperate to please, announcing herself while wanting to take cover. In Bourgeois's own words, 'she does not know that she is half naked, and she does not know that she is trying to hide'.

The figure vibrates with the tension between her desire to be seen and her need to retreat, something I deeply understood. Sometimes the strength of those opposing drives also made me feel like a hybrid creature, a split thing. I could build a whole castle out of my desire to be loved, and I also wanted to be left alone. Sometimes it felt like there were no limits to my wanting, as if it were a devouring and insatiable force. I looked for proof that other people felt the same, and found solace in a letter Simone de Beauvoir wrote to her lover Nelson Algren in 1947,

> I want everything from life, I want to be a woman and to be a man, to have many friends and to have loneliness, to work much and write good books, and to travel and enjoy myself, to be selfish and to be unselfish . . . You see, it is difficult to get all which I want.

I wanted to recover and I wanted to be free, not yet able to see that they could eventually be one and the same.

The duality of the *femmes maisons* made me think of other oppositions I knew well, the archetypal contradictions of the addictive personality: grandiosity and self-loathing, neediness and rejection, confidence and insecurity. (When I later talked about this with my mother she pointed out that I could also be describing the archetypal personality of the artist.) Drinking – or any other addiction – smooths out the jagged transitions between these alternate states. Without it you have to suffer the agony of wobbling between the two, until in recovery, ideally, you eventually learn the path to equilibrium. But the wobbling feels terrible and you think you can't cope so, often without knowing what you're doing, you reach for a replacement fix – a cigarette or a doughnut or a man from the internet or a new pair of blue snakeskin shoes. And for a while it works, and feels good. But it doesn't matter what you reach for to fill yourself up, anything you use as a fix leaves you empty in the end.

In the meetings I'd heard people use the metaphor of six dustbins and five lids to describe the way the addictive person-ality refuses to be contained – you wrestle the lid onto one aspect of it only to find that another is left open, its messy innards spilling out. Because most of the time addiction doesn't really go away, it simply moves house.

I found mine would cycle through a series of things: smoking, sugar, sleeping, shopping. Television and work, though in a world that values productivity over almost anything else no one worries too much when you get addicted to the latter. I was getting better at recognising when my relationship to these things crossed the line from neutral to addictive behaviour, but I couldn't always tell while in the grip of it. I withdrew obsessively into my thesis, reading and rereading the stories of the women in the Salpêtrière, prisoners or patients depending on how you looked at it (we were all housewomen now). Lost to the clamour of a history whose echoes I heard clearly in the present, in my own expe-rience of alcoholic breakdown and in the general response to women in distress: the ancient mistrust of our terrifying emotions. All of us, women on the verge of a nervous breakdown.

Every surface in my flat was lost to paper, the whole space turned over to the task of trying to solve an unsolvable puzzle as I manically poured out the contents of my mind. I cut my hair short and observed the changing shape of my body – fuller, softer – as if it were happening to someone else.

Some days were filled with a perfect solitude; others, my loneliness left me breathless. But a retreat is not a disappearance, and loneliness is not lost time. In the words of the poet Ocean Vuong,

> The most beautiful part of your body
> is where it's headed. & remember,
> loneliness is still time spent
> with the world.

In my cocoon I discovered that loneliness itself is a teacher. I'd always feared it, though since puberty it kept time within me to a metronome's steady beat. My habit was to rush to escape it, into any of my fixes, or into the consoling salve of approval – it was soothing to my soul to feel well regarded. And so in my drinking I spiralled in a double direction, towards the thrill of rebellion and the succour of acceptance. I wanted everything; it was difficult to get all which I wanted. And the gold stars of validation can only ever cover up the cracks. As the *femmes maisons* know, they don't do away with your duality.

In the silence of my paper nest I listened for the familiar beat and all it was trying to tell me: that still I did not feel at home in my body. That my inconsistencies still demanded my attention.

Meanwhile, small but vital details continued to crumble from the edges of my father's knowledge and time began to feel more like the enemy than ever before. It was not skin he was shedding but fragments and facts, things essential for reading the world: letters, names and gestures. Nouns were becoming slippery things, numbers too. The only thing generated by his chaos was confusion.

While my attempts to become responsible, to develop my inner *senex*, had led me to batten down my hatches too thoroughly against pleasure, my father only wanted to eat ice cream and apple pie. He no longer remembered the names of old friends but the hot cross bun song was seared indelibly into his mind and he would gleefully sing it at random: *hot cross buns, hot cross buns, give 'em to your daughters, give 'em to your sons.*

It was surreal to be swapping roles – at first it felt like a game. I'd always loved my father's playful side, his rebellious streak and deep love of the absurd, and these were things the changes in him brought to the surface. But he had also always been a steadying presence in my life and I was afraid of losing my anchor. He'd been quite strict when I was young, during my teenage years the five-and-a-half-decades between us yawned wider than ever and for a while we struggled to understand one another at all. That changed once he saw me as an adult and we settled into a loving and largely accepting dynamic. We disagreed about plenty (politics, music, a sensible bedtime) but we trusted each other and I loved him.

He pursued a life different from the one he was born into

and his career meant my life was shaped by the kind of bourgeois privilege many who hold it are quick to disavow. As a child I took it for granted, and as an adult, though my feelings about it have always been complicated, I've remained profoundly grateful for the security it has given me – my father encouraged me to go my own way, and his generosity meant I was able to.

In the wet January of 2016 my father was diagnosed with mixed dementia. Alzheimer's was a word even less welcome than alcoholic and it landed in our family like a meteor: that I had seen it coming for a long time did nothing to mitigate the devastation when it hit.

My mother and I tried our best to adjust to the unpredictable pace of the disease. At the library my piles of books about hysteria were eclipsed by my piles of books about dementia. I learned that in Alzheimer's disease, as in alcoholic blackouts, the hippocampus is one of the first areas of the brain to suffer damage. This is why forgetfulness and an inability to form new memories are often the first symptoms – as though one's guardian seahorses get disorientated and are no longer able to keep things in order in the brain.

I knew the terror of lost time and I wanted to protect him from it, though there was some comfort in the thought that I understood a little of what he suffered.

One understanding of addiction is that it's a disease that stems from the neurological, the genetic, the biological and the environmental. Some of us are predisposed and often it runs in families. There's a broad spectrum of severity, too, from so-called high-functioning addicts and alcoholics whose external lives are barely affected, though they have inwardly collapsed, to those who fall completely out of their own worlds. Many of us die, and like everything in life, the odds are rigged. If, as I did, you have the safety nets of whiteness and financial security, the university, close friends and a family you speak to, you are likely to be caught by at least one of them on the way down, and held by their combination as you claw your way back up. Choice feels more possible when you're not in perilous freefall or when your privileges mean you have less to lose.

Others believe the labels 'addict' and 'alcoholic' are stigmatising and only serve to hold people back from developing self-control, which is all that's necessary to recover. Others still believe addiction is a sign of moral weakness and those who succumb to it do not deserve any help at all.

The experience of addiction is often one of finding yourself invaded by a primitive force that bypasses who you think you are in the service of its own satisfaction. The more you act out, the stronger the force gets, creating new internal pathways to lead you away from pain. Like desire lines in a meadow, these pathways get worn deeper with time until eventually they replace the full and complex map that had built up over many years. Recovery is the process of creating new pathways in different directions, but the old ones never disappear completely. They may grow mossy and harder to see but it would only take a handful of trips back along their seductive trails to re-establish their monopoly. Whereas in Alzheimer's, pathways start to disappear and reappear at random, and once they go there is very little you can do to restore them on purpose.

But while Alzheimer's and addiction are both diseases of forgetfulness, one has the potential for recovery and the other has no cure at all, moving only in a single, terrible direction.

Now we had a name for the deconstruction at work in his mind, my father found himself bound by a new set of rules: no keys, no car, no going out alone. We locked the front door from the inside like guilty jailers, ashamed of ourselves, waiting for him to realise he was trapped.

I think I'm losing my marbles, he told me one day at golden hour as we sat in the conservatory eating apple pie. His gaze was fixed on the view of the garden: trying to conceal his nervousness with a smile, he told me that there were monkeys in the trees.

The aim of meditation, I remembered the Buddhist teacher saying, is to calm the disobedient monkey mind and learn to observe it without judgement. It was clear my father was not judging the monkeys but his observation of them was uneasy because in a different part of his mind he still knew only he could see them. What kind are they? I asked him and he said he didn't know. I wondered if it was a vision of what he was starting to lose, as if the monkeys were pouring out of his mind and playing in the garden before they ran away.

In an empty window quite some distance away across the neighbouring gardens he could also see a face watching him at all hours of the day, which troubled him much more than the monkeys. Do you see them? he asked me. There, half hidden by the curtain?

My only solution was to try and make him laugh. On my

next visit I brought him a big jar of marbles but he didn't remember what he'd said about losing them. For the next few years they sat on the hall table like a taunt.

Before long a new expression started to settle on my father's face, one of optimistic simplicity and total vulnerability. It was comforting to think of what was happening to him as a slide back towards some kind of childlike state, but the truth was less consoling than that: at first, loving someone with dementia is more like watching sinkholes open up inside them right in front of you. Somehow you have to accept constant uncertainty.

It was around this time that the future became a sudden and powerful obsession: more than anything I wanted to know what would happen. It was not a feeling I was used to. But watching dementia in action changed how I thought about time. A terminal diagnosis brings death out of the abstract and into sharp focus, and when that terminal illness slowly eats memory, even more so.

Who are we without our memories? And if they disappear before the rest of us, what's left? *What happens if you drop all the things that make you 'I'?*

Dementia also changed how I thought about identity, and the meaning of the self. At this early stage in his illness my father looked the same as ever, and if you didn't know him well there were few indications that he was out of sorts. That's what it's like at the beginning – a disorganisation of the building blocks that make a person who they are: their memories, their skills, the things they know about the world around them. They are them, in the process of becoming not-them, like a familiar reflection in a mirror that's cracked.

I'm reminded of a popular line from a poem by the giant of Argentine literature, Jorge Luis Borges: 'We are our memory, we are that chimerical museum of shifting shapes, that pile of broken mirrors.' You're as likely to find it as the epigraph to a philosophical discussion of selfhood as you are in the classic format of shareable inspirational quotes on the internet – superimposed over a picture of mountains or the sea – because it makes sense to people. Most of us understand ourselves to be complex and evolving entities shaped by our experiences over time: as the also much-repeated line from Walt Whitman's *Song of Myself* goes, 'I am large, I contain multitudes'.

The thing is, it's comforting to believe in a unified self. Though we change as we grow and develop there is solace in the sense that our child selves exist in continuum with our young adult selves, our middle-aged selves and eventually our old ones. The idea is that we grow in wisdom and experience – from *puella* to *senex* – and we learn from our mistakes, but there is still some essential 'us-ness' that carries us through from cradle to grave. Memory is one of the ways we hold onto it. Stories are another, the accounts we give of ourselves and the versions of us they cement in the minds of others. Really, all we ever have is an impression of who we are, made up of our hopes and beliefs about ourselves, our denials and repressions, our habits and obsessions, and the versions we see reflected back by those around us. Often if we don't like what we see, we change our mirrors rather than ourselves.

So what happens when a person stops being able to tell their own story? Memory and narrative are what give us a sense of wholeness, and the lost time of alcoholic blackouts and the lost time of dementia are missing bricks in the construction of a coherent self. For the addict, the drive towards oblivion is partly the drive to escape from the self, to forget everything and live, at least momentarily, purely in the now. Free from baggage – you, but unburdened by your history, and your pain. You, flying through the warm night on a stranger's motorbike. You, and the volcano that could erupt at any moment.

I tried to see what awaited my father in this way. As his disease progressed I knew it would claim ever more of his autonomy and independence, but maybe it would also take him towards a different kind of freedom, one of unencumbered consciousness. It was a nice idea but my fear made it hard to believe in. I was faced with one simple, primitive fact: I just wanted my dad.

It was a feeling that welled up in me at unpredictable moments, triggered by things that I struggled to make sense of. I didn't yet understand this was the beginning of grief. Memories of long-ago things would appear out of nowhere and wind me with their vivid strength.

In particular I was haunted by the first time I was forced to confront my father's mortality. When I was ten, his heart gave out. He'd been having chest pains, news my parents protected me from as I'd just started at a demanding new school and they believed it would all be fine in the end. But an allergic reaction to the dye test to check for blockages stopped his heart completely and he was rushed into emergency surgery which narrowly saved his life. Ever since, the spectre of his death had calcified into my most profound fear. As I grew up it was the void into which I poured every anxiety – there was a part of me frozen at ten years old that believed I would never survive it.

Now, seemingly at random, I found myself transported to that day with uncanny clarity. In my mind's eye there I was in the office of my new headmistress, wearing my favourite red T-shirt with Rebel Rebel printed on it and ripped jeans that my new friends and I had doodled all over in blue pen during science class, certain I was there to be told off. Instead she was kind (though I remember she raised her impressive eyebrows at the doodles) and put me into the black cab that had been sent to collect me. When I arrived at the hospital everyone smiled with the tight determination of adults pretending that everything would be all right. A patient young doctor showed me a plastic model of a heart. It was life-size, and seemed huge. I remember its red and blue veins and arteries, and running my fingers along the smooth sides of its chambers. I tried to imagine the hearts of everyone I loved, and wondered if they all looked the same. The word *bypass* seared itself into my vocabulary.

Traumatic experiences shatter the illusion of a coherent identity: they split your life into a before and an after. Addiction and illness create a similar schism: between self and addict, between wellness and sickness, between person and patient. The time before the descent, and after.

The surgery took many hours and the man who emerged was older and thinner and yellower than my father. His eyes were dull and he smelled different – sour and clean. Eventually we brought him home, where he began his long and slow recovery. He had faced death and now he was changed. I would sit with him on the sofa in the conservatory, where he was surrounded by the green of the garden outside, and try to make him smile. And afterwards as if in a trance I would walk to the newsagent at the end of the road and use my pocket money to buy any of the sweet things in colourful wrappers that lived just below the counter, as I had already learned that for a moment they would make me feel OK.

These assaults by the past only served to feed my new obsession with the future. The unknown felt intolerable and I wanted to find out what was coming next. As the magnolias were bursting forth all over the city in a flirtatious chorus, I went to visit a woman who I came to think of as a sort of white witch (though she would never have described herself that way). She lived near the river at the green edge of the city in a leafy, distant place and I would knock for her when the call of the spiral woman swelled up with the familiar pressure of a craving.

She offered what she called intuitive counselling. Hers was a long way from the riotous aesthetic of the New York City psychics with their neon and gold, their velvet and Tarot cards, but in essence what she offered was the same: the comforting illusion of certainty in the unknown.

Her white flat was full of white things and during our readings she poured weak tea from a white teapot into dainty white cups on their dainty white saucers. Lavender scent filled the air. In the gentle glow of candles I listened as she talked of twin flames and new paradigms and future happiness she knew would find me. The sing-song of her soft but assertive voice held my attention.

Before I got sober I was certain of many things. Now I was startled by the heft of my ignorance, and it left me open to paths I would never have considered before. AA proposes that the solution to an addict's problems is to find a higher power, and though I could never quite manage the idea of God, the meetings chipped away at the granite of my atheism. So did the magical thinking that comes with loss.

The white witch explained that her words channelled an energy of consciousness with access to more information than us. The old me would have rolled her eyes; the new one leant forward in anticipation. They say there's a real hope within you, she told me, but that it's split into pieces. For so long you've been stuck but they want you to know that you're in a period of enormous transition and they celebrate you for all that it took to get you here.

She told me what I wanted to hear: that my father was not suffering, merely moving into a different phase of experience. I longed to believe her but I knew it wasn't true; I'd seen the pain and shame and fear that sometimes flashed in his eyes and I knew there was no way through his disease without them. But I liked the idea of being celebrated by an energy of consciousness that knew more than I did, and in the warmth of the candles and the sweetness of her praise I found respite from the clamour of the worlds both inside and outside my mind. Here was another place where tenses could collapse. In her words, past, present and future folded together into a picture of blissful coherence where everything had meaning and was leading to something better. A soft, seductive trap.

Eleutheromania

THE FOURTH YEAR SOBER

Reality is a sound, you have to tune in to it not just
keep yelling. – Anne Carson

IN THE SUMMER OF 2016, I didn't think reality was a great
place to be. My father's health continued to get worse and
the UK was pulling itself apart in the debate on whether to
leave the European Union. I was gloomy so there was never
anything in the fridge. Everyone was talking about freedom: the
freedom to leave, the freedom to stay, the freedom to have a say.
I thought about it all the time too – life felt heavy and I longed
for abandon. It was a time when I ate a lot of biscuits.

That freedom means different things to different people was
never more evident to me than in sobriety. I kept thinking of
all the times I must have passionately described the ways I
liked to get free to someone for whom they sounded like the
opposite.

The night of the Brexit vote I stayed up till dawn watching the results come in on my phone, texting friends in different time zones. When it was announced my eyes were dry and moleish from lack of sleep and I felt part of my identity had been stolen. It is heartbreaking, said a message from Kate in New York. I cannot fucking believe this, said Steve from Toronto. I just woke up into hell, I replied. It was my third sobriety anniversary.

On the first day of my fourth year without a drink I was full of nostalgia for a life I used to live. At the back of the crisper drawer in the bottom of the fridge I found a sad-looking apple and bit into it in front of my laptop at the rickety kitchen table, sitting on a chair that was too low to be comfortable. I had four of them, the kind of mid-century wooden ones that were trendy at the time, which I thought I'd found for a steal on eBay until they arrived and I saw they were child-sized, designed for a primary school, which was why they were so cheap.

I opened the photos folder and searched for pictures from my previous life as a European citizen. The computer organised them by date, which was helpful to someone like me with an inability (and an unwillingness) to situate themselves in time. The folder 2007–8 documented the year I spent studying in Madrid, and 2010–11 the year I moved to Paris for a university teaching job.

We'll always have Paris, Wormtongue said. *Even if you stick with this recovery nonsense. You've never been sick, just attention-seeking. You'll get over it eventually.*

I'm not listening to you today, I replied. But I didn't know how not to hear him, and the echo of those words sounded in my mind until nightfall.

I studied languages because I imagined I'd forever be able to move freely around Europe, for work and for pleasure. It was one of my trusted escape routes and I'd taken it for granted all my life. When I first learned French and then Spanish I discovered they were doors into different realities, and it thrilled me. Though I was too undisciplined to really master their grammar I loved the different identities I found in them – rowdier in Spanish, more refined in French – and the new worlds they opened up. Speaking in their different sounds it was easy to leave myself behind. When I got bored of being where I was I would put my phone on silent and pretend to talk into it in one borrowed language or the other, to practise my accent but also to pretend I was living a different life: *oui oui, c'est moi, j'arrive. Hasta pronto, cielo, ya vengo.*

In my kitchen I ignored the news and scrolled instead through image after image of my twenty-one-year-old self as she careened around Madrid. I liked the way her shaggy, short-fringed bob framed her young and open face, and felt a strange vertigo wondering what she'd think if she could see me now, certain she'd be disappointed. Where was the glittering academic career, the books with my name on their spines? Where was the apartment in New York, with its wardrobe full of glamorous things? Where was the feeling of having arrived?

The pictures from Paris I remembered better as they were more recent, though the twenty-four-year-old woman who appeared on my screen still looked to me like a different person, dressed in moth-eaten vintage and a *Dr Zhivago* hat, with vampish red lips, her arms around an endlessly rotating cast of characters – colleagues, friends, would-be lovers, strangers in bars.

Told you we had fun, Wormtongue said, seizing on the hot pang of envy I felt for the carefree young woman in the pictures.

We did have fun, I replied, it's true. We did have a lot of fun.

My thirtieth birthday was only a month or so away and I didn't know how to feel about it. Written down, the number looked like an accusation – it made me think that I was lucky to have made it and also that I had wasted a lot of time.

No Thirty Under Thirty lists for you, said Wormtongue, who that morning was on a roll. *Shame you missed the boat to be a Bright Young Thing, would have been a gift of a pun.*

The truth was I was both sad and relieved to leave my twenties behind, now that it turned out eternal girlhood was not freedom but just another trap.

Looking at the photos I knew they showed a time in my life when addiction was settling in but still I preferred to remember it as full of the good kind of chaos: the highs and lows of that intense trans-European first love; wine-fuelled discussions long into the night with new friends where total nonsense was argued passionately until our faces hurt from laughing; skipped classes, dancing to exhaustion in sweaty clubs, dawn walks home. The busy streets of Malasaña at closing time, the Canal Saint-Martin at dawn. When hangovers were an excuse to roam the city floating just above myself and there were no real consequences, at a time when the future felt infinite and a long way away.

Though as I got further through the albums, I noticed an

unavoidable shift. There were more pictures where my eyes started to look blank and vacant, my gestures frenzied, often blurring the frame. Smiles became grimaces and I could see I was alive with a manic intensity that was unsettling. Then there were large chunks of time without any photos at all, ellipses from the depressions that stretched longer and the days spiked by anxiety that peaked higher and more often and sometimes meant I didn't want to leave the flat at all. Missed days of work and cancelled plans. The feeling of always letting everyone down.

I clicked on with my mouse and there came darker memories still: the time I fell backwards down a marble Madrid staircase and knocked myself out, ironically saved from worse than a concussion by the fact that my body was floppy from drinking; or when I stumbled home along the canal in Paris and a man pushed me against the door to my building and shoved his hands up my skirt as I fumbled to key in the entry code. I took a bite of the sad apple and stood up from the table to try and shake off the mental images. They were not things I wanted to recall.

In the albums from my years in Madrid and in Paris I could see the same pattern repeating. At first, in the early pictures, I'm ablaze with optimism, high on the excitement of being in a new place. Then, as time goes on, the gloss of it wears off and evidently I turn to other things to cure my restlessness. My drinking gets heavier, my depressions get deeper, my anxieties get more relentless, honed into an excruciating, neurotic self-focus that separates me from everyone and everything. Things start to unravel. The path of my addiction was never a linear one but a spiral that spun in both directions, sometimes towards contentment, sometimes towards chaos. With every spin, the spiral's orbit got a little wider, reaching for a bit more mania, a bit more disarray. For years I could balance the spinning well enough to get through my life relatively unscathed, until the orbit stretched so far that I couldn't.

That year in Paris my depression got heavy enough that some days I couldn't imagine a future at all. I applied for the PhD so I could put off thinking about living the rest of my life, and disappear instead into a world of art and ideas, absorbed by an institutional structure that broke the future down into only the next four to five years. I could just about conceive of that. What would happen when I finished it was beyond my comprehension.

Now, my thesis deadline was only months away and Wormtongue was relentless in his campaign against me: *You can't do it, you know you can't. You'll fail the viva, they'll finally see you for the lazy fraud you are. Give up give up give up. Give up and have a drink.* What stopped me was nothing more noble than bloody-mindedness. Wanting things was agony, especially with him around, but I knew the fear he traded in kept me stuck and I longed to find a way to escape him for good. And now, the more relentless he was, the more my determination was honed by anger.

Often it's easier to feel anger than fear and in the weeks and months that followed as I worked to finish my thesis I raged at many things. I raged at the impossible weight of patriarchal history and the sexist legacy of hysteria. I raged at the labels I felt constricted me and I raged at the sight of the milk-fed men in power, at their navy suits and school-boy haircuts, their smooth faces and pale hands. I chose righteous causes for my anger, but I raged with such intent and such fury that eventually I wondered if it was rooted in something else. If maybe it was also because I was lonely.

At first, when I eventually relinquished the fantasy crush from the meetings, to my surprise I found something wild and limit-less in the refusal of romance. A letting-go, an opening-out, a still, deep lake with nothing lurking at the bottom. It gave me the chance to redirect my attention, and to rediscover the power of choice. I'd been scared to step out of the economy of desire – measuring your worth against admiration for and from others is a habit it can be hard to get out of – but it wasn't long before a profound sense of liberation took root. I felt freer than I had for a long time.

I had also stopped visiting the white witch so I could try and tune back into the sound of my reality. Avoiding it had got me into trouble before: the addictive cycle of craving, consumption, high, then low, are all different ways of yelling, to borrow from the poet Anne Carson's imagery. So far recovery seemed to be about tuning in even if the sound you heard wasn't one you liked. It was hard, but I was slowly getting better at it.

It's a strange paradox that abstinence, with all its restriction, can bring about freedom. Before getting sober I was wary of anything that could be viewed as puritanical because of the way society has always policed women and queer people, especially when it comes to sex. I've never thought of pleasure as a luxury, but as a human right, and while it's still denied to so many people, self-denial seemed like a strange decision. But compulsion is the thief of joy, and what I'd learned in my recovery so far was that if something gets complicated, abstinence from it can buy you space and time to figure out why. Compulsion lives in the moment – the word *now* is its oxygen. Agonising as it tends to feel at the time, if you can let the moment pass, other possibilities will open up, and this in itself is a kind of freedom: room to reflect on what you actually want, instead of just acting on blind impulse. In recovery I learned to shift the focus from what I would lose onto what I might gain, like the chance to speak the truth about myself to myself, which is another way of feeling free.

Living alone, mostly working alone, I enjoyed the impression of total self-sufficiency. I lived under the illusion that I was now a balanced and reasonable person because I had control over so much of my life. Above all, it was a way of living that didn't risk more loss. It felt good to need no one, as if I'd mastered some human weakness, and I liked going against the grain of what was expected of a woman my age – it was a way to break free from all that I found restrictive about heterosexual narratives and expectations. I'd spent years tangled up in them but they had never quite fitted me and I felt suffocated by everything they came to represent. My attraction to men was the stronger and more practised part of my sexuality but it had never been exclusive and eventually in the stillness brought by celibacy it sank in that the only desire of mine that was ever completely binary was the one to escape my own mind.

But what began as a contented solitude and a restorative break from my romantic life now felt like it was strengthening into avoidance. As if I were braced against the potential chaos brought by love.

And now that my father's losses were picking up speed I didn't feel strong in my solitude, I felt alone in it. Time spent with his gaps and absences was a strange contradiction – we were together but separated by the fact that we no longer shared a reality, and it was lonely looking after him. Because dementia moves those in its orbit in two cruel directions at once, every thought I had of the future was followed by the breathless knowledge that to think forward was also to think of his death. It was why I never had anything in my fridge: to plan even days ahead seemed oddly like a betrayal.

Then there was the guilt. More and more I felt the loss of the things I gave up to spend time with him. The work of caring is as mundane as it is colossal: with dementia, devastating losses unroll to the rhythm of meals that need cooking, washing that must be done, teeth that must be brushed, nails that must be clipped and cleaned. Even when I wasn't with my father, part of my mind remained attuned to his needs. There were days when I felt envious of the friends whose lives looked light and free of responsibilities to anyone but themselves, whose energies, as far as I could tell, mostly went into their careers or having a good time. Sometimes I did not want to see him at all, to avoid what was happening to him, to deny it by refusing to bear witness to it. On those days I bargained with myself, and struggled against the knowledge that my life had shrunk and that increasingly I wanted to escape it. It was easier to be angry about the things I felt I was losing – things that would eventually be retrievable, like a social life or a sense of ambition – than to feel the force of all that had already been lost to the void of his disease.

That October the big news was that America might soon have its first female president. As I raced towards my deadline fuelled by hot flashes of rage I couldn't stop thinking about my father's shrinking memory and my own shrinking life and the solitude that no longer felt like freedom.

January arrived and brought with it more bad news: America's new president was not the woman many had hoped for. Instead he was a cartoon villain whose voice left a sticky trace like snail slime. There was nowhere you could go to escape it – even though where I lived he was not in charge, it poured out of every radio and television in a viscous ooze. Whenever I heard it I wanted immediately to wash it off my skin. I was busy trying to let go of my own internal villainous voice and didn't have room for another one, though I was glad to have one more legitimate target for my fury. One of the paradoxes of grief is it can soften and sharpen you at the same time – just as it rouses your anger, it peels back the protective layer between you and the world so everything permeates and little is contained.

Meanwhile, the voice I did want to listen to was drifting further away. My father's speech had started to falter. I was struggling to face up to what it meant.

Not long before the official naming of his disease I started taking a photo of us every time I saw him. The word 'selfie' made him laugh so we would lean our heads together as I framed our grinning faces in the rectangle of my phone. He was fascinated by the technology, which to him now seemed like magic. When a friend whose own father had died young and suddenly a few years before saw the pictures, she told me that photographs were good to have but what she missed the most was the sound of his voice; she suggested I record our conversations before it was too late.

I was too superstitious to do it right away, afraid that if I started recording he would immediately die, that my capturing of his voice might somehow bring about its silencing. Then I worried I'd become morbidly obsessed with listening to them after his death. But the changes within him were already well on their way and I knew from my reading about Alzheimer's that if he lived long enough to reach the late stage of the disease he would lose his voice completely.

When I made the first recording it was a bitterly cold, cloudless day and he was in his usual spot in the conservatory, on the same sofa where he'd recovered from the heart surgery that had saved his life all those years before, swathed in scarves and basking in the sunlight. He would often sit like that: eyes closed, hands behind his head, body stretched out into an almost straight diagonal. The burnt orange of his sweater glowed, optimistic in the crisp light. I opened my mouth to say hello but as I got closer what I saw meant no sound came out. Something was wrong with his face. His mouth had fallen open in sleep and in it there were at once too many and not enough teeth; his sunken cheeks were distorted. When I managed to call out to him he woke suddenly with an intake of breath, sucking the dentures that had slipped down off his gums back into place and breaking into a sleepy smile.

It's strange to find horror where you expect to find comfort. As always I'd brought him something sweet – two chocolate éclairs from the supermarket, their fresh cream smeared slightly onto the clear plastic window of the box – which we ate watching my mother in the garden talking on the phone, waving her cigarette through the air for emphasis as she spoke. I bit into my éclair and was glad of the sugar and the way it made me feel less afraid.

Determined our time together would not be spent under the shadow of his death, I decided not to tell my father about the recordings. I thought he might guess my reason and worried it would upset him, or that he might ask me not to make them at all. On a tall pile of books on the table in front of us I balanced my phone and hoped he wouldn't notice as I pressed the red record button at the bottom of the screen. We settled into our usual topics of conversation – what the monkeys in the trees were up to, whether someone was watching him from the window across the gardens, whether there was life on other planets (he was always certain there must be and I, like Mulder, wanted to believe). He asked me if the Earth was round, then said, I used to be a scientist, you know. When I suggested a walk he asked if we could take the car. I can't drive! I laughed, and he conceded that neither could he. I don't know why I can't drive, can you remember? Yes, I said, because sometimes you would forget where really important things like the brakes were.

Listening to these recordings now what shocks me most is the intimacy of sound. I can hear my father's body move as he picks up his tea and takes a sip as though he is still sitting beside me. His voice is thick with the dentures that no longer fitted and the shapes of his words get looser in each one as over time his brain becomes further clouded with plaque – his yes becomes a yeah, and sometimes it's impossible to understand him at all. I can hear myself searching for things in him, trying to reassure him while at the same time I desperately seek the reassurance he had always offered me about things beyond my control. Eventually our voices simply jumble together into an abstract kind of nonsense, a kind of father–daughter jazz:

[*big sigh*] [*whispering*]
　　What are you counting?
　　Thirty-one, forty-one, fifty-one, sixty-one, seventy-one, eighty-one, ninety-one, hundred and one, hundred and eleven, what's the date?
　　The date? Is . . . twenty-seventh of March
　　No, what year?
　　Oh ninetee— uh, twenty seventeen [*laughs*]
　　Thirty-one, forty-one, fifty-one, sixty-one, seventy-one, eighty-one, ninety-one, hundred and one
　　Two thousand and one
　　Hundred and eleven, hundred and twenty-one minus four

Eighty-six

I'm eighty-six

You're eighty-six [*laughs*] No I think you might be eighty-five, and about to be—

Yeah

Eighty-six. I think you're going to be eighty-six in August

God

Do you feel eighty-six?

No

How old do you feel?

Ninety-six! [*laughs*] No no

How old do you feel in your mind?

Um. About sixty

The oldest person registered on the planet is a woman in Jamaica who's a hundred and seventeen. Can you imagine?

Yes I can. I wouldn't want it.

At the time my visits to him in the conservatory felt like a performance I gave several times a week. My persona was one of limitless patience and mirth, with little trace of the anger and frustration I let myself feel when I was alone. Back at my flat, I would disappear into work for hours every day, barely stepping into the world at all. I slept little and ate strange things at strange times. My excuse was my deadline, but there was a perverse freedom in that kind of self-neglect: if I could forget my body I could forget myself and that meant I could forget my sadness too. I could escape into letters and words and the *tap tap tap* of my keyboard, which was often enough to silence Wormtongue, though the minute I stopped I knew he'd return, peddling his guilty reproaches.

Life then was staged in a procession of rooms and when I think back on it now I imagine myself as a character in a cross-sectioned set, moving between them: my rooms, my parents' rooms, the rooms of the Salpêtrière. It was a life of interiors and an interior life, and this narrowed context made the choice to stay in recovery easier at a time when I was vulnerable to rejecting it. If I kept things tightly controlled there was no space to question the roles to which I had decided to commit – those of recovering alcoholic, caring daughter, diligent researcher. I gripped onto them tightly as you might cling to a rope thrown from a pier while a current threatens to pull you out to sea.

'Don't let your solitude obscure the presence within it that wants to emerge,' writes the poet Rilke, who, like Simone Weil, believed in the liberatory potential of going down into yourself. 'Precisely this presence will help your solitude expand.' In the ten letters to Franz Kappus (at the time a nineteen-year-old aspiring poet) that make up *Letters to a Young Poet*, Rilke lays out what he considers important in life, which, as well as to do one's creative work, includes solitude, love and to do difficult things. I love how he expresses the constant dynamism of human experience: 'Everything in nature grows and defends itself in its own way and against all opposition, straining from within at any price to become distinctly itself.'

Eventually, through my anger and my sadness, the presence

within my solitude that wanted to emerge revealed itself as an impulse to move my body and to be out in the elements, to walk a long way in the open air without stopping. It was a call towards the natural world that I had never before felt so strongly. I wanted to put my body where life unfurled without intervention, to move under a big sky and through green spaces, to feel connected to the rhythms of life that continued to beat regardless of all that was difficult and sad. What emerged from my solitude was a desire to let go, and most of all, to let go of Wormtongue. I wanted to know how I could finally leave him behind.

When I travelled 200 miles down to the Cornish coast, the first grey strands threaded through my hair and my thesis was in the hands of my examiners. It was May 2017 and I was overcome by the kind of eleutheromania that used to lead me into trouble.

Eleutherios, which means liberator, was another name for Dionysus, the Ancient Greek god of excess and wine. When I drank, that's what I sought – liberation from everything I found difficult and tedious and hard to bear. And maybe the myth of Dionysus is proof that the urge to slip off the constraints of a civilised life and get free by getting high is a very old one, old as humanity itself. But now I was looking for a different way to indulge it – to find abandon without abandoning myself. I hoped that a few days walking beneath rolling skies and beside the unbounded sea would be the answer.

Look at you, Little Miss Hiker, Wormtongue said. *A regular recovery cliché.*

I tried to ignore him but there was something in it. By then I'd been around meetings long enough to know that for a lot of people there suddenly came a point in their recovery when they became enthusiastically, compulsively interested in the natural world. As if they'd never noticed it before and then – bam! – it was all about the grass and the trees and the light touch of the breeze, as though it took them to the same highs as whatever they were in the meetings to let go of. If I'm honest that's probably why I wanted to give it a try.

The train to Falmouth demonstrated I still had much to learn about delayed gratification. Looking out of the window as we sloped through Devon under a heavy grey sky I started to see snatches of sea, mudflats, the distinctive red of West Country soil. Steep drops and tall pines outside of Liskeard, old stone houses. Flashes of ultraviolet snapped past as we picked up speed among the foxgloves and the view blurred into a marble of green, mud red and grey.

As if to test the intolerable itch of my impatience, at Par the train stopped for ten full minutes. Through the window I saw a little girl and a man loading their surfboards onto a VW van. He was young, fit, lightly bearded, with long, tangled hair the same blonde as the girl's. When they turned towards me I saw they shared a face, she an uncanny, miniature copy of his sharp-edged features. I thought of my own father's fragility, of our matching hands, and longed for something to chase the feelings out.

Go on, said Wormtongue, *get a beer from the trolley when it comes round. You could handle it. Just one wouldn't hurt. You've been working so hard. You deserve it.*

Restless, I shifted in my seat and turned the volume up on a podcast so I could drown him out. The sardonic voices of two American women discussing the brutal nineties murder of four teenage girls filled my ears and for a while I half-listened as they described the crime scene — a Texas yoghurt shop — but found I didn't have the stomach for it and turned it off. *Just one wouldn't hurt.* Maybe one wouldn't, but it was never just one. And in my unsteady spiral into dependency I had learned that anything you dispatch with a drink or a drug will be back with reinforcements at twilight. I reminded myself that in recovery what I'd chosen was not the avoidance or denial of difficult feelings, but to develop the strength to learn how to face and then tolerate them, which really was a kind of freedom, even if it didn't always seem like it. Still, Wormtongue's words tugged insistently at the heavy, padlocked door in the back of my mind.

In my wallet I remembered there was the three-year sobriety chip that I had collected in June. Its outline was visible through the teal leather like the circular ridge of a condom. Protection of a different sort, I thought, and dug it out so I could have a proper look at it. Bronze, slightly tarnished, it was lightweight and reminded me of a token for a fairground ride, or playing Pogs in the school playground at lunch. At its centre was the number three in Roman numerals: three proud sticks like Doric columns at the entrance to somewhere sacred. It reminded me of ancient coins.

As long as we've had systems of barter and exchange, coins have been about freedom. Which means freedom has been something that, in theory, you can buy. Only I found the mechanisms of capitalism to be one more relentless trap. I was still susceptible to anything that promised to change my mood and had all the regrettable online purchases to prove it: sometimes things would arrive that I couldn't remember ordering (and that I definitely couldn't afford), and I would send them back, spooked and ashamed of myself. I wondered what kind of middle of the night trance I must have been in, locked into the demanding glow of my phone screen and whatever solutions it offered me: the shoes of an efficient woman; pots and pans that would make me a chef; stationery for my new virtuous and productive life.

It's the trick of an inflated ego to think everything is about you, but having an addictive personality can make it feel as if the contemporary world is designed to dial into your weaknesses. Everything is geared towards consuming more: Netflix binges, flash sales, the urgent imperatives to change your life by buying this one specific thing. In fact, looking at my little bronze prize, I could see that the addictive impulse and capitalism were actually very well matched. They both work to commodify things. They both drive you to think in terms of what something can do for you, or how it can change the way you feel.

I often wondered if the only way to peace might be to leave the city and become a hermit, answer an ad like the one I remember seeing for a hilltop shrine in Catalonia that was looking for a caretaker. Though I wasn't exactly handy, and for that one you had to be 'pure of spirit', which I was pretty sure counted me out.

Around the outer edge of the chip was stamped *To Thine Own Self Be True*. It sounded good to me but I wasn't sure how to do it with Wormtongue always in my ear. Truth is a slippery concept when there are two of you.

These days of walking promised a break from the noise made by advertising's empty enticements, and maybe a way to quieten the voice inside my head. I hoped I might recapture the peace I'd found on Stromboli, and emulate the glamorous philosopher, who I hadn't forgotten. She came to me in visions that felt like visitations, her calm presence in my mind a welcome counterpoint to Wormtongue's constant belittling agitation. You always have a choice, she'd tell me, even when you think you don't. You are usually more free than you feel. I began to think of her as some kind of benevolent deity and wished I could summon her at will – my own secular goddess of freedom.

The Roman goddess of freedom was called Libertas, and coins were minted with her image. In Ancient Greece she was known as Eleutheria, which was another name for Artemis, goddess of the hunt, complementing Eleutherios/Dionysus. Symbolised by the crescent moon and the bow and arrow, in Greek mythology she's a protective and sometimes vengeful deity who oversees moments of transition and changes of state. She's especially associated with childbirth and the shift from youth into maturity, like a divine midwife mediating between the wild and the civilised, between life and death. I've always liked the sight of her in classical paintings and sculptures, proud and strong and surrounded by wild animals, a quiver of arrows on her back. Independent and on the move. Maybe the Greek goddess and my Strombolian philosopher were related.

I like that in the mythology Artemis and Dionysus are corresponding figures. Both of them are wilderness deities who stand for different kinds of freedom: Dionysus represents the liberation found in intoxication and wild abandon, while Artemis embodies the freedom of the chase. She was known for freeing female slaves, and her vow of chastity meant she avoided marriage and childbearing (she was immune to the powers of Aphrodite), which liberated her from the traditional expectations of her gender.

I was drawn to the idea of her, and you can learn a lot by noticing the stories that hold your attention. The philosopher Mary Midgley describes myths as 'imaginative patterns, networks of powerful symbols that suggest particular ways of interpreting the world', and like Jung's archetypes, they offer templates for making the mysteries of human nature more intelligible. While Artemis offers a vision for women different from the one grounded in societal tradition, Dionysus shows us that it's normal (maybe even divine) to revel in excess, to seek communion through intoxication, to feel a hunger for transcendence and for abandon. Both show that these aren't impulses to be ashamed of.

If you're someone who has tipped over the edge into self-destruction and compulsion this can be an important thing to accept. In the fragile months of early recovery it's easy to be too extreme and cast the whole experience as negative, sometimes it's even necessary in order to commit to the change. For me, it countered the impulse to mythologise, something I am mindful of again now as I write this – the ego loves a good story. But with enough safe distance from the behaviour, with less fear of it, I could see things more fully. I understood that the impulse for transcendence itself wasn't to be feared, that sometimes it was even a good one, I just had to choose carefully what I did with it: for now, the path of Artemis – of walking in the wilderness – was for me a better bet.

But you don't even have the right shoes, said Wormtongue.

I looked down at my boots, a new pair of the same red ones I'd worn out that first winter without a drink.

What if you're a myth I can choose not to believe in, I snapped back.

'The first step in recovery,' writes Craig Nakken in *The Addictive Personality*, 'is the acceptance of the dual personalities created in addiction.' Acceptance is different from disbelief. As Simone says, you must accept the void. Accept the voice that comes from the void. Wormtongue was my voice from the void, and it was no good to simply pretend he didn't exist. I had submitted to him, ignored him, argued with him. Accepting him was the one thing I hadn't tried, and I decided maybe it was time to.

Multiple personalities are supposed to be a sign of insanity, but even when things got very messy and I was afraid I was losing my grip on what was real, I never really saw myself as mad. It was normal to have an inner life, I told myself. It was normal to talk to yourself. But maybe an inner monologue is different from an inner dialogue, especially one with a voice that undermines you and encourages you to take ever bigger risks. Or turn your back on your life completely.

A smiling man with deep laughter lines rattled into the carriage pushing a trolley full of things to eat and drink. Anything I can get you? he asked, as I looked at the jewel-bright line-up of miniature bottles: whiskey, gin and vodka. Tea, please, I replied and dug out some coins. I never used to like tea but now, like a national cliché, it seemed I drank it all the time. When he gave me my change I picked up the bronze chip that still lay on the table and ran my finger over its raised surface one last time before, along with the pennies, putting it back in my wallet.

At first I was dismissive of the chips. I thought they were pointless, embarrassing even. But a reward is a reward and as the days, then weeks, then months of my sobriety stacked up it didn't take long before I started to look forward to collecting the next one. I discovered that when you've lost something as abstract as a sense of yourself, it's useful to have some physical proof of its restoration. Which is why on my first sobriety anniversary I bought myself a ring cast from magpie bones. I hoped it would ward off sorrow and point me towards joy, and I'd see it on my hand if I was tempted to reach for something that I now understood would do me harm. It would remind me of what I'd found once I'd got my feet back on steady ground – the longer I stayed sober the more I learned that addiction is a disease of forgetfulness not only when it's active.

Even in abstinence, I discovered that the addictive part of me worked to protect itself. Which was why recovery needed to be an iterative process, something I had to do rather than something

I could just think about. It couldn't be static – even its dictionary definition emphasises something that happens over time: 'the action or process of regaining possession or control of something stolen or lost'. Sometimes the process was good, sometimes it was painful, sometimes it was extremely dull and excruciatingly repetitive. That day I missed the enthusiasm I used to have for it when I first started out.

Finally we pulled into Truro, where I had to change trains. The new one was much smaller, like a cheerful little caterpillar, less busy and more noisy in a jolly sort of way. I let the rhythm of its wheels lull me into an ever more reflective mood.

The first AA meeting I ever went to was recommended by the kindly psychiatrist, and was in the basement of an imposing church in a smart part of the city far from where I lived. What I remember of it comes in flashes: the solid wooden door that I hesitated to push open; the boyfriend who came in with me when it looked like I would bolt; lots of strange faces; freshly pressed jackets; shards of light in the dusty air; stackable chairs. At the end everyone held hands and recited a prayer, which made me want to run. But the strong-looking man who sat at the front of the room and narrated his experience of addiction and recovery said a single phrase that pierced my defences. He had a 'washing machine brain', he said. An overwhelming jumble of thoughts and voices and urges that only quietened when he escaped into drink. I knew exactly what he meant.

Seeing as I promised the psychiatrist I would go to three before I made up my mind, in spite of my strong reluctance I went to another meeting the following week. Like all newcomers

I was told to listen for the similarities and not the differences, advised to get a sponsor and to work through the twelve steps. It is helpful to find a higher power, people told me. Try to accept that you're powerless and find a way to surrender.

I wasn't sure about any of that but I was desperate to feel different, to feel better. To begin with that was enough, even though I was suspicious of the zeal the fresh-faced people I met seemed to have for a substance-free life. Their kindness unnerved me, as did their enthusiasm for hiking. I identified more with the quiet and the shell-shocked who sat at the back, fidgeted throughout and bolted the minute the meeting was over. In the scrolls that hung on the walls the word God featured heavily and made me uncomfortable. I didn't believe in one, and wondered often whether AA was a Christian cult (Google said yes and no, depending which links I clicked).

But as I listened to people tell the stories of what had happened to them, the meaning of the word 'alcoholic' started to change and expand. Its definition grew to include not just the behaviour of excessive drinking, but also the mindset that meant that it felt like the answer. In the church basements and community centres I visited all over the city I met every kind of person — those with everything you're supposed to want and those with none of it. Rich, poor, delinquent, upstanding. Religious people, angry people, unstable people, famous people. Those whose needs were desperate and those who seemed to have it all worked out. Some had only been sober for days or hours, while others had over twenty years stretching out behind them.

It took a while to get used to the language they used, which at first seemed patronising, banal and repetitive, but, when I could quieten the churning of my own mind enough to listen to whoever was speaking, what I heard was the same story I knew well: a person struggling against the demands of their addiction. It was in meetings where I first heard about intrusive thoughts, and where I met other people who really got what it meant to think in terms of 'we': *we need it, we must have it, we deserve it, we can't live without it.* There I met people who knew how it felt to live alongside another voice, one that loved you when you indulged it and loathed you when you didn't. How do you break up with a part of yourself? I wanted to know. Like most dysfunctional relationships, it was hard to quit.

Occasionally I thought of the question asked by the man with the electric shock machine: where, exactly, is the source of your pain? Sometimes the why of addiction is something you can point to, a catastrophic event or a life lived in the shadow of intolerable trauma, but for many of us who wash up in the rooms of recovery it's nothing so direct. Drinking was a good solution for an intense and sensitive over-thinker like me (thin-skinned, my mother used to say, and, knowing life can be hard on the sensitive, urged me often to grow a thicker one). But long before I had a drink, when I was just a child, reality wasn't really where I wanted to be. Imagined worlds always struck me as better.

Most importantly, what I heard in meetings over those three years helped me to understand that Wormtongue hadn't only appeared that first restless, sober winter. It was just that, once I stopped giving him exactly what he wanted, his yelling had got loud enough to take on a voice of its own. Before then he had spoken in cravings and impulses, disguised as desires that pulsed through my body like hunger. As I fell into addiction those desires became needs and the sense of another force acting within me started to grow stronger. Recovery was a way of understanding that force and learning to accept it. Maybe it was also a path away from that voice, back towards an integrated sense of self. Though he didn't stop yelling right away, I hoped I could follow the path far enough away from him that I could tune back into the version of reality I had known before he got so loud.

It was late afternoon when the little train finally pulled into Falmouth station. I stood up and stretched my legs, excited to get where I was going.

When I got to my bed and breakfast on the harbour I dumped my things out on the enormous double bed: not enough clothes and too many books. I was new to this sort of thing and wasn't sure what I might need so I repacked my mother's old brown leather backpack, with its cracked and ailing straps (it had been the most practical bag I could find), with the most sensible things I could think of: a bottle of water, some Savlon, some plasters, a bar of chocolate, a packet of Camel blues that I planned not to smoke, a yellow lighter, my green notebook, a pen, some lip balm, my swimsuit and a bright blue sarong. I must have eaten something but I don't remember what. Mainly I recall being excited and a little nervous to get out on the path — walking the city you can stop any time and hitch a ride on a bus if you get tired or it rains, but out here I'd be alone and at the mercy of the elements. I tied the laces too tight on my Doc Martens and shoved a grey blanket scarf into my bag just in case.

When I set off in search of healthy ways to escape it was humid and warm. The sky was grey and the empty beach looked like crusted brown sugar. At first I walked with a novice's gait – tentative on the uneven ground – but I soon found my pace as I followed the green trench cut by the narrow path as it snuck past the bay.

The South West Coast Path is a 630-mile route tracing England's southernmost edges. It wraps around the counties of Somerset, Devon, Cornwall and Dorset, where it began as a way for the Coastguard to patrol for smugglers: they would walk from lighthouse to lighthouse, right at the edge, so they could peer down the cliffs into tucked-away coves looking for contraband. Now it's for walkers and creatures that graze the land. And people like me, with something to let go.

The first stretch was straight and man-made and fenced off by wooden posts fixed with wire: not the wilderness I'd hoped for. Hedgerows full of yellow flowers dizzied in the shifting air and beyond them, a flat grey sea. In front of me the uneven bulk of headlands rumbled down to the water. Everything looked heavy with prehistory. I felt small and ephemeral set against the cliffs and their ancient indifference, which was a relief.

Wormtongue's undermining chatter was incessant: *You should have worn proper hiking boots, you're not fit enough for this, you'll get lost, you'll trip up, you're not a hiker, who are you trying to fool, if you twist your ankle no one will find you, turn back, turn back, turn back.*

I tried not to listen but not to block him out either, to simply let him prattle on without caring either way, as if he were an annoying but not totally intolerable relative. I discovered it was easier to practise acceptance while I was on the move. Slowly the pleasure I took in my moving body began to work as a shield. There was a thrill in driving myself on, propelling my muscles to carry me around the next bend, and the next, and the next. Whatever Wormtongue said, I just kept on walking, and bit by bit the kinetic energy of my body worked to shift my thoughts as well. I felt like an empty vessel gradually filling up with the smell of the grasses and the sound of the waves and the feeling of my feet as they crunched sharp pebbles beneath them.

In the meditation classes I attended at the start of all this, the melancholy Buddhist with the steady voice had also taught us about walking meditation. When we reached the end of the course he said he thought it would suit me in particular. If your mind is too restless to tolerate sitting still, he told me, then instead try moving your body while you practise being at one with your breath. He quoted the beloved monk and spiritual teacher Thích Nhất Hanh: 'When you walk, arrive with every step. That is walking meditation. There's nothing else to it.' I remember thinking then that Buddhists have a special skill for exposing the human compulsion to complicate things.

After years of trying to outrun myself I was in Cornwall to walk at a steady pace, no matter how difficult it might be. I carried on putting one foot in front of the other and counting my breaths in and out, one, two, one, two. I listened to the language of my body, and what it said encouraged me on. As I followed the path my eyes adjusted to the landscape and I began to pick out new shades of green in the hedgerows and varying tones in the sea that stretched out to the horizon. Blue sky gets a lot of airtime but in Cornwall I learned the beauty of a thick white cover, when a flat, bright light calls the other colours to their strongest essence. Against it yellows and magentas glowed neon. All around me were bees drunk on nectar and other insects that buzzed at different pitches and tempos as thick clouds hung overhead, unrelenting. So what if it was unoriginal to quit drinking and take up walking? I was starting to get what people saw in it.

For several more hours I continued without stopping and barely noticed the passing of time. It was as if I walked beyond something within myself, into a new state of calm that I hardly recognised as part of my own consciousness, a feeling of total wellbeing. On the path that day I first understood the difference between the kind of movement that's an escape from the self and the kind that's an encounter with it.

Flanking me on either side were often dense thickets of mugwort. I didn't know much about plants back then but I recognised the jagged sprays of sharply pointed leaves and tall, purple-tinted stems from my reading about hysteria. *Artemisia vulgaris* has for centuries been used all over the world to treat all kinds of ailments (from fevers to stomach aches and chest infections) but particularly as a menstrual tonic. Because it stimulates blood flow to the uterus, it's thought to help regulate irregular periods and even induce miscarriage, and because the root of the hysterical impulse was historically understood to be in the female reproductive system – the ancients believed its symptoms were caused by the so-called 'wandering womb', and that the uterus could actually travel around the body causing trouble – mugwort appeared in various places as a potential cure for hysteria. As I scribbled a quick note about the mugwort in my little green notebook it occurred to me that I was in that moment a good embodiment of the wandering womb.

In his book about the invention of hysteria, the French philosopher Georges Didi-Huberman, whose thoughtful blue eyes were always framed by small wire-rimmed spectacles, writes:

> The Greek hystérikē can be translated by 'she who is always late, she who is intermittent'. Yes, she who is intermittent is the hysteric, she is the intermittent of her body. She lives with the risk and misfortune of always mis/taking the possession of her body. She feels that perhaps it is not hers.

This bodily intermittence was something I knew well, but only now that I was preparing to leave the hysterics behind could I really understand that it also applied to me. My body was something I had spent years finding ways to escape from, caught in a swing back and forth between the false sense of freedom brought on by neglect of it to a sometimes excruciatingly intense presence within its boundaries. But now, as I wandered, I felt no separation between body and mind at all. I was a single entity, all bound into one, and in that I found a deep and unexpected pleasure, and also a relief.

Eventually I had to turn back and with the looming sense of a destination the feeling of total presence was harder to hold onto. It was lonelier on the way back and the closer to town I got the more of a challenge it was to stay with my breath. Wormtongue started up again, as if grabbing me by the hand to drag me off in another direction. His criticisms were harsh as ever but I tried to put what I'd learned about acceptance into practice and simply responded: Oh, there you are. Hello Wormtongue. I was sad to lose the feeling of quiet contentment I'd encountered as I walked but when I got back to my room I slept more deeply than I had in a long time.

On the second day I woke when the moon was still a pale crescent in the dawn, hanging in the sky like Artemis's bow. A satisfying tiredness weighed down my legs and my head was quieter than the day before. It felt good to wear myself out. With my swimsuit under my clothes and a crisp green apple added to the essentials in my bag I struck out in the direction of Rosemullion Head with the intention to walk all day and be back before nightfall.

You should really give this up you know, it's total bull—

Hello Wormtongue, I replied. Hello old friend.

The path was empty in the hazy morning and lit with magic. Dew twinkled on plush verges that reached down to the sea.

Birdsong and sea-song filled my ears in an energetic chorus. How strange that city people like me often say we long for the country quiet, when to be in nature is to be surrounded by noise. It had taken me a day to acclimatise, to recognise the depth in the silence that wasn't silence at all, and now with each step it seemed I tuned in to yet another layer of sound. The cries of birds, some of which I knew – the caw of urban crows is the same as that of country ones – others that were new to me and sounded rasping and prehistoric. The glassy sound of wind through dried grasses. The motor of a distant boat. I felt the expanse around me as each noise resounded fully in open space, with no brick walls to bounce off. I walked on, paying attention to my breath and my steps, and letting the sights and sounds of the landscape fill me up until once again it was as though I had been emptied of all my worries.

The path narrowed to a dirt track framed by hot pink foxgloves, their flowers full of furry bees like winged bears in silken gowns. Crowds of ferns unfurled towards the waves and at the water's edge rock forms spilled out under green thickets and pooled like sticky caramel. In the rockpools were colonies of garnet sea anemones that matched the colour of my boots. My body was warm as I slipped through the kissing gate with no one to kiss, just me and the foxgloves and an edge you could fall off. It struck me sudden as a stroke: I was happy.

Since my father's diagnosis, happiness – the kind that fills you up with a steady contentment, a gentle feeling of wellbeing – had felt out of reach. I'd sought manic highs and their attendant crashes but the peaceful sense that things were simply OK was not something I'd felt for a while. Maybe not since stopping drinking. It was what the first drink promised: an end to the restless irritation, a calming of anxiety and angst, existential or otherwise. A chemical replication of a state of grace, though it never lasted very long. But this feeling of emergence, of contented fullness and absolute presence, this was something else. This was joy. The same kind the poet Emily Dickinson meant when she wrote, 'find ecstasy in life; the mere sense of living is joy enough'.

Years later, in the midst of the Coronavirus pandemic in June 2020 when we were all stuck inside and joy was harder than ever to come by, I read an interview with the American academic and writer Saidiya Hartman that transported me back to that moment on the path. She described joy as 'the sense of the self disappearing in the context of the vastness of the Earth, the ocean, the sky, the land. That kind of joy is always about self-dissolution, escape.' Self-dissolution and escape, things I spent years seeking through destructive channels, when really they were here all along.

I walked and walked until eventually I stopped to rest beside a glut of giant prehistoric-looking plants with leaves that opened out like enormous hands. They looked big enough to take my weight (they were rough to the touch, how I imagined elephant hide might feel) and I pulled my phone out of my bag to take a photo.

There was no reception and I felt a jolt of anxiety. These days I never switched my phone off: my father would often call at strange times with urgent questions – Where are you? Where's your mother? Where am I? – and now the revolving door of hospital visits that comes with old age had begun to spin I needed to be able to talk to doctors and the rest of the family. The smell of wild garlic carried on thick, salty air as I looked at the now redundant shiny black rectangle. I felt panic at being uncontactable, but also a guilty sense of liberation.

A few days before I left for Cornwall my father had rung me and then didn't know who I was. It was the first time it had happened and I felt the blow physically, like a kick to the chest, knowing it would not be the last.

Losing someone slowly while they're still alive is a strange kind of anticipatory grief. The Swiss-American psychologist Pauline Boss calls it 'ambiguous loss', a suspended mourning that stretches indefinitely. Since the 1970s her research has looked at the effects of the kinds of psychological and physical absences that lack resolution – dementia and disappearance, but also addiction – and the unique kind of stress they bring. We think of absence and presence as opposing states, but in the addict or the person with dementia they come together in an uncanny contradiction. The person you love is there but not there, change-able, intermittent in themselves and in your relationship with them. After the finality of absolute loss follows the process of mourning, which, though terribly painful, has a natural logic to it. A clear relationship between cause and effect. But when a loss is ambiguous, this logic is thwarted. How do you mourn a person who is still alive? How do you grieve for a relationship which, though it may be decimated by emotional and mental absence, still technically exists? How do you hold both versions of a person in your mind at the same time, and live with the anxiety that one is usurping the other, even against your will? It is unspeakably hard on the heart.

I crouched down to get a good shot of the massive leaves and saw their stems were covered in spines.

Back on the path the clouds finally drew back on a vivid Formica blue and before long the hedgerows gave way to the golden sand of Maenporth Beach. I sat beside the gossipy waves, a little tired, and tried to find consolation in the beauty all around me. I was distracted by the fact that I wanted a cigarette and also wanted to not want a cigarette. After years of nicotine addiction I was astonished that I now seemed able to be an occasional smoker, and didn't really trust it.

Go on, said Wormtongue, *a reward for all the walking.*

I noticed his voice was quieter and sounded more and more like my own.

Hello again Wormtongue, I replied, and batted away the idea – his or mine I couldn't say – that maybe now I could manage to be an occasional drinker too.

Around me on the beach families played with their dogs and their children – we're playing It, you're It! – ate ice creams, knocked down sandcastles. As I lit the cigarette (it was inevitable) and took a drag I considered this almost imperceptible dice with death, the danger so abstract, so distant you can blow it away on an exhale and not think of it again.

A large white swan glided over the chop like a hallucination. It spread its wings and with a surprising lack of elegance used the thick webs of its feet to run up into the sky. No one else seemed to see it.

I took off my clothes and followed the gentle slope of sand into the sea. Cold water rose slowly up my limbs and pushed between my thighs as I waded deeper. I swam into the blue and loved how it took me out of myself, dissolved my edges and absorbed me into the enormity of its depths. I loved how the sea held the shape of my body, which was older and fuller than it used to be. At my most ill with drinking I'd lived mostly on adrenaline and it ravaged my roundest parts, emptying out my breasts and my hips until I cut a new shape as I moved through the world – smaller and sharper but more fragile, too, with thin, brittle hair and yellowing bruises (then, even the lightest grip would leave fingerprints behind).

The smaller I was, the more approval I got, because women are still admired for shrinking in space. For a while it was addictive to be so well regarded, and approval is a heady drug (especially when you're low on self-esteem, which is an inevitable consequence of addictive acting out). The only group whose attention I lost were the ones I'd wanted to shed since I crashed through into puberty – the men who used to kiss or whistle or spit when I passed them in the street. The kind of attention that can sometimes masquerade as admiration but that, once I was older, I understood to be a toxic mix of lust and rage (genuine admiration rarely leaves you feeling hot with shame). For a while they left me and my slighter, quieter, less overtly feminine body alone and I felt liberated. I grew to love the freedom it gave me to move through the city unencumbered by their gaze and the unwitting physical performance of my gender. And so I became anxious to preserve this new smallness, even if it meant going hungry.

It's perverse that hunger itself can become a fix, with the heady sense of mastery over the body it offers – especially to a body whose appetites have led it into trouble. For a time, to deny myself nurturing food made me feel strong. I can see now, though, that the tightness with which I held onto that denial went beyond my vanity, that it was also a way of feeling the strength of my agency while in another part of my psyche I felt totally out of control.

Once I stopped drinking, my commitment to indulgence soon won out over my commitment to thinness, which struck me then as undermining to the pursuit of so many deeper and more expansive pleasures. My anger at the sexist and racist prejudice against roundness that I'd internalised won out over my desire to be admired primarily for the shape of my body, which, when I really thought about it, seemed like a strange and fickle thing to want. And it's good to really think about what you want – often I discovered it was what I'd been taught to want by the culture I was born into, which is not necessarily the same thing.

Now as I swam, I felt the power in my strong thighs and a new respect for my body, which for years I had neglected and which had recovered from so much. Beside me, I felt the presence of that intense, lost young version of myself, with her bruised shins and her restricted appetite. I lay back and let the clear, salty water fill my ears. All I could hear was my heartbeat. Slow. Things felt effortless and I was free. It was a moment of grace, not the chemically replicated kind or one bestowed by any god but by the luck and life force of being alive. My animal body, unencumbered. Maybe my higher power was the sea.

Here, encircled by the comforting indifference of the natural world, it felt easier to accept complicated things. Cornwall is a place of deep contradictions, where the wealth of outsiders who want to own their share of paradise meets local poverty, and where the bounty of an untameable landscape meets the limitations of crumbling infrastructure and years of political neglect. Around me I saw a land and seascape that could by turns be welcoming or hostile, a place of refuge or a place of danger, somewhere that offered sustenance or somewhere that was itself in need of protection. A place where illusions of control held no sway at all — just like on Stromboli, it was clear that the answer was to surrender to forces far bigger than my own will. And so, while the gentle support of the water reminded me to accept my body, walking the South West Coast Path showed me that it was possible to accept Wormtongue too, that in fact to reject him would be as foolish as trying to reject the creatures that lurk in the deepest ocean crevices where the light can't quite reach. We may be unnerved by their alien appearance but in the complex marine ecosystem they too have their part to play. As Jung wrote, *Wholeness is not achieved by cutting off a portion of one's being, but by integration of the contraries.*

In what was to follow, joy would come and go like the tide, and Wormtongue wouldn't give me much trouble anymore. The critical voice didn't disappear completely but after Cornwall it grew quieter, and I was less in thrall to its pronouncements. They were easier to deal with once the voice that spoke them no longer sounded separate from my own.

Looking back at the gently rolling land, I pulled myself through soft, buoyant waves and tried to imagine the future, finding, for once, that I could.

When I got back I went to the university as a student for the last time. It was the day of my viva and I felt the calm resignation of the jumping-off place, where the only thing to do is let go. My supervisor met me outside and took me to where my examiners were waiting, two men, one in person, one on a screen. Their expressions were mild, their questions rigorous. I hid my nerves behind red lipstick and high-heeled zebra-print shoes, and touched the irregular shape of the magpie ring for courage. We talked about theory and film and the wandering womb and I was grateful that my wayward mind remembered how to fall in line. There was a surprisingly simple joy in realising that in spite of my unravelling, I had worked hard and it had paid off. Or that maybe it was precisely because of my unravelling that I really understood my subject. My examiners asked why I'd included the work of Louise Bourgeois, and as I answered them it dawned on me that the depth of my interest in hysteria might come from a similar place to hers – a curiosity sparked by an intense and sometimes overwhelming inner experience that in turn sparked a desire to figure out how to give shape to the psychological and the emotional, be it in sculpture or in words. I had spent years engrossed in thinking and writing about the line between sanity and insanity, about presence and absence, about women who were there but not there, because I was trying at once to escape and to understand what was happening inside my own mind.

At the end of the hour to my astonishment the examiners said, Congratulations, Dr Bright.

On Margate Sands

THE FIFTH YEAR SOBER

That selfhood which is our torment, and our treasure, and our humanity, does not endure. It changes; it is gone, a wave on the sea. – Ursula K. Le Guin

BUT WHAT GOOD IS IT to be a doctor when you love someone who's sick and there's nothing you can do to fix it? The glow of my good news struggled against my feelings of impotence. All I wanted was to be back beside the sea, close to the constant renewal of the waves and the deep joy that I found there. I was drawn to it as if my blood were filled with saltwater that longed to return home.

Without the structure of the PhD I was adrift, looking for work as a writer for hire and uncertain what to do next. Through trial and often embarrassing error I learned how to pitch editors and built up some tolerance to the cycle of their polite but generic rejection emails, or worse, their resounding silence. My main anchor was the literary podcast and radio show I'd been making with an old friend for several years. Carrie and I had met at graduate school, and she was now a literary agent. Together, each month we would interview a different author, and I was grateful for the way our reading and recording schedule acted as a harness for my newly shapeless days. Letting go of the academic work that had spanned my life before and after getting sober was like shedding yet another layer of my identity. Over the course of my doctorate I learned many things – about critical theory, about philosophy, about how to teach well, about the limits of my ignorance, bureaucracy and compromise, about desire and hysteria and cinema and art – but as I slowly tuned into the sound of my reality I also learned that I'd spent all those years in pursuit of something I didn't actually want. It's easier than you might think to do, when you've always had a Wormtongue shouting, whispering, cajoling in your ear. When your addiction blocks an honest relationship with yourself. Or when you're determined to act as if the future doesn't exist at all. It was only on leaving the bubble of university life that I learned how institutionalised by it I'd allowed myself to become. How reliant on the gold star machine, infantilised, habitually attuned to lurch towards the next pat on the head like a mistreated dog desperate for affection: *There's a good girl.* There was something compulsive in it, that need for affirmation. As though without it I didn't believe I was worth anything at all. Each certificate brought something I could shore against my ruins no matter how desolate I was feeling inside.

Still, without the legitimising authority of an institution I felt nervous and exposed. I was ashamed that this far into my recovery my life wasn't more together, that in fact I still felt lost. Compared to most of my friends, who appeared to be racing ahead with theirs, I felt too slow on the uptake and longed to be back by the tide with its steady reminder to keep on letting go.

When I got a libretto-writing job that took me to Aldeburgh on the Suffolk coast I saw it as an omen that with my sea fixation I was on the right track. My collaborators were a young French soprano and an English filmmaker and our home for the residency was a small pink cottage with pale roses around the door. We were there to devise a one-woman show about identity, living between two languages and how possible it ever is to really speak the self, something that was often on my mind with the ebb and flow of my father's waning ability to speak at all. Our first night we stayed up talking among the tall hollyhocks growing in the garden, but I was distracted by my sadness and longed to get in the water so I could try and wash it away. At sunrise I was so eager to get down to the beach that I forgot my swimsuit and ran over the loud grey stones with nothing on. There was no one around and the silver waves were freezing cold. I screamed before I went under.

The next day a few metres down the beach I saw another woman doing the same thing. She arrived on the stones in a towelling dressing gown which she flung off before diving in, and was there again on the third day, and the fourth, and each time we waved to one another from the water.

At the time I was coming off the antidepressants I'd been on since my first visit to the psychiatrist. For years they rescued me from the clenching listlessness of anxiety and depression and provided some steady ground from which to tackle my addiction and complete my doctorate. I'd been on them once before, after an experience of severe depression in my teens that still haunted me, but never for this long a stretch. Now that my sobriety was solid and the PhD was finished we agreed that I no longer needed them, and I said a thankful goodbye to the kind psychiatrist I had been seeing every three months for the past five years, and who had made such a difference to my life.

The slow process of withdrawal was jittery and tough on my body, but it was a graduation more hard won than any of my academic ones and I was proud of what felt like proof of my progress. Something concrete at this stage of my recovery, when, now I was into my fifth year without a drink, the label 'alcoholic' felt like it no longer fitted (to be a sober alcoholic is to live within a strange contradiction). It was a revelation that each morning before work, instead of taking a pill I could plunge into the North Sea: the icy shock did as much to restore me as any chemical compound. It was then that I started to think seriously about moving to the coast.

On the last day of the residency the sun blazed so bright that after my swim I walked along the shoreline to let it dry off my hair. I soon came upon the giant sculpture of a shell that sits facing the waves, one half propped up by the other lying face down on the stones. It's called *Scallop: A Conversation with the Sea*, a tribute by the artist Maggi Hambling to the composer Benjamin Britten, who had lived in Aldeburgh. Each day he'd walked that stretch of coast; now he was buried in the graveyard a few steps from our cottage.

Cut into the steel on the upright part of the shell is a line from Britten's opera *Peter Grimes*, which tells the tragic tale of a fisherman and the aftermath of his apprentice's death at sea: *I hear those voices that will not be drowned.* The words sprang hot tears to my eyes.

My father loved opera. He'd taken me to see a production of *Peter Grimes* not long before he started to change, and the power of it had left both of us awestruck. My whole life he'd filled the house with the music he loved, but now his mind was too far gone to follow it and he preferred silence. In the shadow of the giant shell, my hair still dripping saltwater onto my shoulders, I thought of his voice. How, for all our efforts, it was drowning. How the erosion of dementia is a tide you cannot halt. I thought, too, of Wormtongue, whose voice was now folded into my own. Not drowned exactly, but assimilated, and less powerful. It's easier to stand up to a monster when you know what shadows it's made of.

After that the sea spilled its way into my thinking. As I faced the uncertainties of the next part of my life I aimed to be like water, fluid and flexible and open to change. I said yes to whatever work came my way and went to the coast whenever I could: in July, to Dungeness, where the stony beach is a strange landscape of brightly coloured shipping containers and boats, tangled nets and jaunty buoys, where a friend and I ignored the NO ACCESS signs as we took in the detritus of a hard-working shoreline, and afterwards in my green notebook I wrote: *Today*

I went to Dungeness, now all I want is to go back to Dungeness, and dream of sulky Dungeness; in August, to County Mayo in Ireland, where I stayed with another friend and we swam every day in the freezing Irish sea, and bathed in warm saltwater and seaweed at the baths in Enniscrone, emerging sylph-like from the deep stone vessels that held us along with thick tangles of bladder-wrack, our skin smoother than it had ever been, and where I celebrated my thirty-first birthday, and hoped to feel like a grown woman at last; in September, to Brighton, where I marched against Brexit with hundreds of others dressed in the rich blue of the European flag, my swimsuit underneath, and where I was reminded that I preferred my beaches deserted.

Like Goldilocks, I was trying out different coastlines for size – this one too far away, this one too windy, this one too wild, this one too tame. Of course, though I couldn't see it then, I was up to my old tricks, trying to drown out my feelings with a new sensation, a new place, the glimpse of a new life. I came to the sea the way I came to a drink, looking for something to ease my discomfort. All I knew at the time was that the threshold between land and water, between the known and the unknown, was where I most wanted to be. I began to wonder if it was possible to be addicted to the sea.

Before I could find an answer, my father collapsed and instead I learned it was possible to drown inland. He was rushed to hospital in a frenzy of blue lights and alarms. When he got there his ward was full of people sliding fast towards death. I felt the acrid tang of fear in the stale recycled air. Over the beds, instead of numbers there were pictures of spring flowers and it was odd to see them fixed above the wilted bodies of people in the winter of their lives. He was in Rose bay and in the next bed, beneath an improbably vibrant picture of a hyacinth, lay a person so small that their mattress could have been empty save for a tangle of sheets. I watched a porter wheel a shrouded body through the ward. He was a ghost no one wanted to see. As he passed, the nurses turned their shoulders as if against a chill. The patients seemed not to notice him at all.

Sitting beside my father under the bright hospital lights I thought about the meaning of recovery. There, I could see the flaw in my desire for a sense of continuous progress, which can't help but suggest a perpetual movement towards something better or a destination at which you can arrive. Sometimes recovery is not about moving forward but about being able to stay still. I listened to my father describing things only he could see and understood that although on the end-of-life ward the only concrete progression was towards death, it was still a place where people could make small recoveries along the way. Somewhere they could recuperate, and where convalescence might buy everyone a little more comfort, and a little more time. I was afraid that time for my father was running out.

Meanwhile, in a trick of fate that made me feel like a character at the mercy of a writer with a cruel taste for ironic symmetry, a version of my father's hallucination about the face in the empty window that watched him from across the gardens came to pass in my real life. While I was becoming fixated on the sea, a man who lived opposite had become fixated on me. For a long time I'd been working hard to ignore his attention, but its escalation meant that the dam of my denial finally burst.

What started with neighbourly waves hello grew over time into his constant surveillance. Before, during the couple of years I shared the flat with my first love and, after that ended, with a friend, the man opposite had paid us no attention at all. His interest started only once I lived there alone, not long after the friend moved out. (She left about a month before the motorbike accident, exhausted by the accelerating chaos of my drinking. As a child of alcoholic parents she could see what was happening, and she did not want to be cast as an enabler to my addiction. She was right to leave, and I often wonder if I would have stuck to the decision to get sober had she stayed.) I'd felt uncomfortable about the intensity with which the neighbour watched my windows for over a year before I first said it out loud. I didn't want to believe it was happening, so initially I ignored the small changes I made to my behaviour in order to avoid his everpresent gaze. I pretended to be on my phone every time I went in or out of my front door so he'd have to leave me alone, and ate my meals sitting up on the kitchen counter with a cupboard door open to block his line of sight. For a long time I imagined I was being paranoid – the legacy of time spent doubting whether I could really trust my own perception. Eventually the man's presence at the window was so constant it could no longer be denied. Looking back, I think my compulsion towards the sea was partly because in front of a wide horizon I felt totally unobserved.

Once he began shouting threatening things, I listened as two plainclothes policemen stood in my kitchen and told me this was a familiar story that never ended well. There's very little we can do, said the taller one (brown leather jacket, frayed-hem jeans, rubber-soled shoes), until a more serious crime is committed. For example, said the smaller one (black leather jacket, frayed-hem jeans, rubber-soled shoes), the sexual or physical assault that is the likely form of escalation in this kind of situation. If you can leave, they said, then you should. I had already started to pack up my things.

That December I moved back to the house I grew up in. I was rattled and looking for safety, but it also meant I could help look after my father. It would be easy to manage my work around his care – I was getting more commissions but still rarely enough to fill the whole of my days, so it seemed like a good solution. Besides, when afraid or in pain, to believe in your own importance gives you the illusion of control. If I could make myself useful, maybe I would feel less precarious. And time moves differently at the start and at the end of a life – just as no one wants to miss a baby's first words, with the advance of my father's dementia I lived in horror that I might miss his last ones. It was as though I believed my being there all the time could stop it from happening. As if my new title – which in the face of his illness felt comically absurd – actually qualified me with the healing powers of a real doctor who could fix everything. If not reverse the damage then at least halt it. Stop the ride, I want to get off.

So for a few restless months during that sad and heavy winter my mother, father and I tried to click back into the triangular shape we were used to. By this point we were all fragile and found that the ratios were off – since we'd last shared a home, too much had changed and trigonometric logic no longer applied. Our dynamics were skittled: the patriarch was now the dependent; the child, however reluctantly, had grown up; the mother was now more like a parent than a lover to her partner of over thirty years. The vortex of my father's rapidly growing needs caught us all ever tighter and we spiralled helplessly towards its centre, where I knew there would be no respite at the eye of the storm, just a stifling vacuum.

With a long and slow disease like dementia you can sink yourself so deeply into the needs of someone else that it's two lives, not one, that are lost to it. This, I think, is a lesson learned by most who become carers to people they love. For me, it was a reminder that just as some addictions are more socially accept-able than others, self-abandonment can come in many guises. In my case codependence is often as compelling a crutch as any substance.

With this realisation I met the limits of my altruism. It's true that caring for my father was an infinitely more useful way to escape myself than some of the other things I had tried, but it soon became something that I did instead of, not as well as, attending to my own life. Eventually I saw that I was using it as a noble reason not to square up to the things I was still afraid to face. Namely, now that I had decided I did want to live it, what I was going to do with the rest of my life. I fought hard against the undertow of my fear that I was going backwards.

For a while, my relationship with my mother was reduced to logistics and stiff conversations about my father's decline, and in our sadness we neglected the rest of it. Sometimes, we fought wildly against the invisible forces that were playing havoc with all our lives and when we did we would collide, with our different ideas of how best to proceed with his care. I know now we were each protecting the other from certain truths we felt would be too painful to bear, but back then we were tired, and anxious, and afraid, and it was hard to always be generous. Nothing brings chaos to a family quite like grief. Our frustration had to land somewhere and because we couldn't hurl it at the disease that was decimating the man we both loved, occasionally we hurled it at each other. For a time, it wasn't just him we lost, but one another too. It's terrible that in a moment of stress an unkind word can feel like a catharsis.

For his part, my father was becoming a more difficult patient. Paranoia meant he grew suspicious of things that were designed to help. He'd tear off the patches that delivered medication supposed to ease some of his symptoms, and although he was now worryingly shaky on his feet, refused to use the elegant walking stick we got for him. I started to find small, colourful piles of pills nestled between books on the shelves or at the bottom of vases holding flowers that died suspiciously fast (it turns out lilies don't like donepezil). Though his ability to be rational was lost, these acts of defiance in the face of the swirling inevitable were small ways he could feel the comforting shape of his agency, which was something I understood.

The weeks unspooled their monotonous chaos of lost things: teeth, glasses, sandwiches, people. I learned how to tread the line between persuasion and manipulation. He was now too frail to do much by himself. While he let me help him with most things there were certain boundaries he wouldn't allow me to cross, one of which was helping him in the bathroom. I think it was a relief to both of us – it allowed me to stay in the role of daughter instead of fully crossing over to the role of nurse. But as he careened towards total dependency it was harder to respect his dignity and keep him clean and safe at the same time. I pretended not to know about the incontinence pads I collected each week from the pharmacy, and was haunted by an unshake-able feeling of failure.

Those months were a period of exactly the kind of sustained emotional stress I was sure in early recovery I wouldn't be able to withstand without drinking. And yet I did not relapse. I don't even remember being particularly tempted to drink, though there was always plenty of alcohol in my parents' house. I did have to grit my teeth against cigarette cravings; I desperately wanted to smoke, all the time, and I fixed on sugar and binge-watching *The X-Files* from start to finish. But by then it seemed that the line I'd drawn under drinking was solid enough that it felt impermeable.

I've since thought a lot about why, and I believe it's largely down to the comprehensive support I received early on in my recovery. When I first got sober I was enrolled at a university, so I had access to excellent and – crucially – free mental health care. The treatment on offer through Student Psychological Services meant I never had to pay to see the psychiatrist or for the medication he prescribed, and the first eight sessions with my therapist were covered. After that, I was able to keep seeing her for years at a low student rate. Had none of that been the case, like most people I met in recovery meetings, I wouldn't have been able to afford either option, let alone both. My own desire to feel better and the help on offer in the rooms of AA (which is free to attend) were two extremely important factors in my getting and staying sober, but they're only part of the story.

Recovery from addiction is an intensely individual path out of an uncannily archetypal experience, and there is no single way to do it. Relapse is a common part of the process and something in which there is no shame. I also imagine it's something fewer people would go through if there were more avenues of treatment available to those who want to recover. As they teach in AA, sobriety is always something it's wise to take one day at a time, and there's no guarantee I won't relapse in future. But I think the fact that I didn't, even in the midst of so much pain, was because by then I had been restored to some kind of reliable equilibrium by a combination of properly prescribed psychiatric medication, talk therapy and twelve-step meetings. Together, they made it possible for me not only to get out of the hole, but to stay out of it, even in times of intense emotional strain.

Proximity to death can also offer an astonishing clarity. As I tried to walk beside my father while he approached the end of his life, it finally hit me how close I'd come to laying waste to my own. How careless I'd been with it. Watching his body grow more fragile by the day, I longed to feel strong and vital, as though somehow I could carry enough life force for both of us. It was a powerful desire and I think it worked as a force field against any whispers from the void.

Winter drew on and I was glad when we passed the solstice and the brief cluster of sunlit hours would slowly start to stretch longer each day. My father was too frail for the cold weather and the risk posed by the icy ground so we stayed inside, but it was hard to spend so much time at home in the dark. As the empty trees looked ever more skeletal, it became clear to us all that we needed more help, and we started interviewing carers. My father resisted but it was half-hearted. He was wary of new people and detested being babied, but at the same time he seemed to understand it was a necessary next step. Over the two months that followed I watched a rotation of mostly patient and mostly gentle strangers as they interacted with him, and felt a complicated mixture of guilt and relief. It was painful to see him struggle against their help, and painful to see him acquiesce to it. I was grateful for the much-needed support from people qualified to do the things my mother and I could not, and the things my father would not allow us to do, but ashamed, too, at how quickly my thoughts turned to leaving. By the middle of February I'd made up my mind to follow the call of the sea.

Two and a half weeks later I arrive in Margate looking for a fresh start, excited to see what I'll find there. It's the third day in March of 2018 and the grey horizon melts right into the water: there's no more edge to jump off. My friend Andrew – who has a kind heart and a driver's licence – drives me and my things down from London in a van and when we get there we eat pea fritters from a chippy on the seafront. I love the crisp salty crunch of batter, how it cracks open to its bright green centre, soft and sweet, a garden taste. A bright new flavour for a bright new chapter. On the beach the sand has iced over. Like a broken mirror, it shatters loudly underfoot.

I'm glad to be here but I feel like I'm on the run, like I've run too far and also not quite far enough. By train, I can be at my parents' house within a couple of hours so I can still help out with my father each week, and I hope the psychological separation I've struggled with will be easier with a bit of physical separation to bolster it. Most of my work I can do from anywhere with an internet connection and if I spend one night a week sleeping on friends' sofas in the city I can make it to recording sessions for the podcast and manage to do the rest. But even so, on the first day of my new life you could say I am all at sea.

The next morning I am woken not by gulls but by the sound of insistent fucking, which starts before the birds can wake up. My new upstairs neighbour's bed is clearly right above mine and it's thudding across the floor with determined enthusiasm. Immediately I feel voyeuristic because fucking is hard not to listen to whether you want to or not, so even though it's early I go in search of a coffee and some breakfast to bring back to Andrew, who is still asleep. Walking around my new neighbour-hood I grasp for the familiar high brought on by the novelty of an unknown place and pass a café so full of plants its entrance is like a portal to a distant, jungled world. Next door is an abandoned shop front that its curly scripted sign tells me was once a *Bridal House and Photography Studio*, but now its windows are blocked up with a grid made by the red and white crosses of eight St George's flags. There's a pottery studio, an escape room and a purple-fronted *Private Shop*, its windows covered for modesty, offering their wares to a different kind of pleasure seeker. There's an organic shop that looks like it serves one community and a little further up, behind windows plastered with images of frothy steins of beer and cured meats and cheeses, it looks like the vast Polish supermarket likely serves another. I drink it all in, excited to once again be somewhere different, still waiting to feel the high of it and quietly dejected when it doesn't really seem to work.

I buy some pierogi and sauerkraut to eat later and keep on past the turquoise-fronted Arts Club and the barbers and the old-fashioned bakery where a sign says you can get fresh quiche and iced buns. Past a run of second-hand furniture shops with mobility scooters out front and the huge windows of a place called Thornton Bobby with retro signs promising *colour television rentals, pianos, records, organs*, though all that's displayed beneath them is a row of old white fridges, which I imagine to be full of hearts and lungs and brains. I find a nice-looking coffee shop that also sells records and buy two flat whites and croissants from the tattooed, lilac-haired barista, who has a warm and lopsided smile. I smile back, and can see why people sometimes call Margate 'Shoreditch-on-Sea'.

In 2018 this neighbourhood, Cliftonville, is in the midst of a slow regeneration. Developed in the nineteenth century as an upmarket alternative to the rowdier parts of Margate, like most British seaside towns it has been neglected for a long time. Now, as well as the immigrant families that have been settling here for years (and the locals who voted against their arrival), it serves a new community of artists, artisans and writers. Many are 'down-from-Londoners' like me, looking for a different kind of life, drawn to that curious mix of pleasure, leisure and reckless-ness that in England you so often find beside the sea.

Breakfast, I say to Andrew who I find on the sofa looking out at some gulls that are jostling bits of rubbish on the street below. The flat has the grand proportions of Victorian seaside architecture: high ceilings and a big bay window that lets in lots of daylight. The main room is too big for my mismatched second-hand furniture, which sits in the middle in an awkward cluster, looking oddly lonely. It faces the green overgrowth from the back of the parallel street's gardens and I chose it because it is not overlooked.

After Andrew sets off for London I unpack more of my boxes and stash most of them under the bed in case I want to leave in a hurry. Over the two I keep out I throw a piece of magenta fabric and balance a large plastic-framed poster of a bird on top to make a coffee table. My stomach is tied in anxious knots but I try to remember the words of a wise friend who always says that fear and excitement present the same way in the body. I choose to feel excited instead of afraid.

Against the long living room wall is a fake fireplace with a kitsch electric hearth made of plastic coals that glows orange when I switch it on, like a piece of doll's house furniture. Though

I haven't tried to meditate for a long time, on the mantelpiece I dutifully arrange the glass jar of Strombolian sand, the incense, the naked woman riding a winged horse in the bright red frame and the candles. The blue skull doesn't fit so I put it down beside the pretend fire, and lean the print of *Summer Days* against the wall on my desk, using the copy of *Gravity and Grace* as an anchor. I open it at random: *We must get rid of the illusion of possessing time*, says Simone.

In 1943 Weil ended her short life by self-starvation in a sanatorium not that far from Margate. At thirty-four, she was only two years older than I am and I wonder if her presence has somehow echoed across time as a way of proving her point. Maybe she knows that out here on the edge of things it's what I am trying to do – pause everything so I can catch my breath. Take time in my hands as if it isn't the same as trying to hold onto water.

Assembled in these new surroundings my talismans look to me less coherent and I feel a long way from the young woman they once represented. Maybe she's gone, a wave on the sea. Maybe I want the tide here to drag in a new one.

And so in the weeks that follow I try my best to start building a life. I spend time with some old friends who made Margate their adopted home several years before, and occasionally take their young son for a spin along the boardwalk. They introduce me to lots of people and I go to events even though I am nervous. I play at being someone whose spirit is light and airy and tentatively I start to make new friends, people who don't know what I'm running away from, people to whom I can pretend I'm not running away from anything at all. For a while I even start to believe it. At one party, under giant golden balloons filled with helium that spell out FUCK I play pool and flirt with strangers, and in a rush remember the electric thrill of a fleeting two-way desire. At another, a love-themed club night, I wear my red see-through dress and think of New York. I dance until dawn under glitter balls and pink lights in a crowd of exquisite bodies painted up in nautical drag. This is it, I think, swaying to the music. This is the answer – no part of me is anywhere else but here, nothing else exists but now. I want the night to last forever, and let the beat move my hips like a pair of strong hands.

This is the first time I've moved somewhere new since I stopped drinking. Without the mask provided by so-called Dutch courage I discover I'm less extroverted than I thought. Before, it felt like I rarely said no to an invitation, but now socialising often tires me out. Sometimes, even if I feel lonely, I don't want to do it at all. I become aware of a social anxiety I'd previously barely registered, a self-consciousness from which there's now no easy escape. But I realise that as a way to meet strangers who might later become friends, dancing is a good substitute for drinking. I prefer it to a night spent in a bar or a pub, where there invariably comes a moment in which everyone else slips towards drunkenness and I feel a combination of things: a disorientating sense of separation as they slow down and I do not, as though I'm on the other end of a video call from the rest of the room and the reception is bad, so the sounds and images don't quite match up; frustration at the broken connection; the tug of a desire to join them in their fuzzy edges; a seductive nostalgia that isn't to be trusted (*nostalgia*, a word with its roots in the Greek for homecoming and pain – homesickness, as if, for the addict self, to drink is always to come home). It's much easier to be in places where the shared experience isn't only drinking, but music or movement as well – gigs, club nights, parties.

And so I say yes to nights of dancing and no to nights in bars and live mainly for the daylight hours. I cook badly and try to stay on top of the washing up. Mostly I live off soups and jars of sauerkraut from the Polish shop eaten with the thick rye bread they sell there. Slowly, a life full of good intentions starts to take shape, designed to keep me busy enough that I don't think about things back home. I go to 7 a.m. yoga classes and try to accept the limitations of my body, though they irritate me and awaken the critical voice in my head. Every morning before sitting down to work I walk past the house with the yellow roses and the one with its curtains always closed and the shiny Rolls Royce that sits outside the most dilapidated house of all, right down to the concrete slip road to say hello to the sea.

As I acclimatise to my new town I begin to notice its different tribes and try to figure out where I fit in. There are the art kids with their neon hair and '90s-style outfits, the music industry types in their well-made vintage workwear, all clearly transplants from elsewhere, like me. Then there are the young families and the older couples and the elderly nursing home residents, the ageing rock stars – one of whom I often see cycling along the clifftop path on a tricycle, towed along by his Alsatian puppy and with a rollie resting on his lower lip – and the lycra-clad wellness practitioners, the stylishly turned-out journalists and the local teenagers who smoke weed down by the waves. Wherever I look I feel like an outsider. I'm still able to be distracted by the newness of it all, but there start to be days when I feel the sharp sting of loneliness and wonder whether coming here was the right thing to do.

One humid morning when the clouds sit unnervingly low in the sky my friend Finn visits and we run around on the long stretch of sand near Palm Bay. Her bright red curls are livid against the soft green lichen that streaks across white rocks making them slippery underfoot. She's excited by the landscape and we walk along the coast further than I've yet been by myself and I'm reminded how much more fun exploring can be when you are two. When she gets the train home I try not to let myself feel bereft, but I do.

Now I can focus more of my attention on pitches I'm getting more commissions, and slowly I start to feel less anxious about work. One of my new friends is writing a book about women's health and several days a week we meet at the jungled café, share a table and write side by side. On the days she isn't there the owners are sometimes the only people I speak to. My voice always sounds strangely loud, and I worry I'm being over-familiar, that my desire for connection makes me seem desperate, eager. Days like that I post pictures of the beach on social media to prove to myself I exist. I don't want to be the sort of person who counts the likes, but I do.

Reinvention is a tantalising prospect when you feel sad or stuck, but it's not something that happens in an instant, no matter how fervently you might wish it would. In Margate, it didn't take long for the new to become familiar, and once its powers of distraction wore off I was left facing the fact that again I'd come to a place expecting it to make me a different person, or at least to make me feel better. It was a lonely realisation, a feeling that somehow I was always the last to know. And as always, when my perception was no longer clouded by what I needed to be true, I could see more clearly what was real. When I looked around me, as much as I saw a neglected town steadily coming back to life, I also saw that its contradictions were getting more extreme. How the influx of new arrivals brought with us that tricky combination of optimism and exploitation that often shows up when a place goes through a rapid shift in identity. There were many ways to live in Margate, and they seemed to rarely intersect.

In the language of addiction, the phrase 'people, places and things' usually refers to potential triggers for relapse, but at this stage of my recovery I could see that for me they were also things I could use as a fix – to escape from difficult feelings into a person, a place, or the promise of a new thing was a more benign version of the same old pattern. The impulse to abandon reality for a fantasy of a different kind of life. Just like in New York.

Believe it or not, there's the faintest echo of New York in Margate. You can hear it at Dreamland, the retro fairground on the esplanade. In 1919 it was bought by a theme park impresario who renamed it after one of the three original amusement parks that stood on Coney Island in the early 1900s. Luna Park, where I spent my twenty-eighth birthday with Kate and Jo, is still there but in 1911 the Coney Island Dreamland burned to the ground. I missed the life I'd imagined for myself across the Atlantic, but somehow this fragile thread of connection was a comfort, as if in some small way I hadn't abandoned it completely.

Spring came on slowly and it was excruciating, with its wet skies and thick mists rolling in off the sea. I spent much of it on trains back and forth to the city for work chairing events and interviewing writers, and to see my father, feeling deflated. My visits home were painful and I felt torn between two lives. I wondered if maybe I was finally growing tired of the queasy thrill of new beginnings.

As T.S. Eliot so famously wrote in *The Waste Land*, April was a cruel month and by the end of it in spite of my best efforts I was tired and I was blue. *The Waste Land* has a special legacy in Margate. In the autumn of 1921 Eliot composed the fifty lines that eventually became 'The Fire Sermon' while looking out over Margate sands. It's a piece of writing I know well and have always loved. Less so the poet himself, though it's easy to imagine him there, gazing down on a beach full of playing children and wounded soldiers, embodiments of the playful and troubled parts of the self that wash up in seaside towns. That spring as the crocuses battled to surface through the frost I felt newly connected to the despair and mysticism of his vision, except my despair didn't feel poetic at all, just relentless and very dull. Now that I could no longer blame it on Wormtongue, I was starting to see it was the grinding monotony of unresolved grief which I was trying, and failing, to leave behind.

Eliot came to Margate in recovery from a depressive break-down after he'd been advised by doctors to leave London and convalesce beside the sea. The poem's disorientation reflects his state of mind – it falls apart and puts itself back together, seeking connections, wanting to understand. It moves in two directions at once, reaching beyond its own edges just as its third eye turns inward to spy on itself. It demands you surrender yourself to it, and then, as Eliot himself once said, recover yourself again, knowing that the version you recover is different from the one you offered up to begin with. I thought often of the poem while I was in Margate, and realised that I now saw in it something else, something new. In its collage of different voices and moods that cut across each other like a radio changing frequencies, I found not only the echoes of my own mutable, polyvocal inner life, but also of dementia, which makes a wasteland of the mind:

> On Margate Sands,
> I can connect
> Nothing with nothing.
> The broken fingernails of dirty hands.

I came to Margate to chase the contented peace I'd found on the South West Coast Path, where what emerged from within my solitude was a desire for connection, even a tentative desire for love, but I caught myself instead in a perpetual dance across the line between solitude and loneliness. Solitude is sustaining but loneliness is a dangerous state for a recovering addict. Isolation (spiritual, mental, physical) creates the perfect conditions for guilt, self-pity and obsessive negative thinking to flourish, all of which are nourishment for the part of you that wants you out of your mind. (As I write this I can hear the psychiatrist, who always used to say at the end of our sessions, Remember, Octavia, for your addict there are only two options: drunk or dead.) Although I no longer heard Wormtongue as a separate voice, it didn't mean the feelings and thoughts he expressed were gone. Now I had to reckon with them as part of myself, not something that could be expelled or bypassed but something that had to be tolerated and accepted again and again and again. There was no other voice to argue with or obey or blame, and there was loneliness in that, too. In the new feeling of really being alone inside my mind.

There were plenty of people in my life then, as I swung back and forth to London on the train, meeting Carrie at the studio to record the show, interviewing writers I admired, meeting with editors, visiting my parents, even flirting with a possible new romance. But the strange thing about the memory of the loneliness I felt then is that it edits them all out, or rather, the times that felt the most real to me were the ones spent alone. In the flat the loneliness seemed to expand into the space, as though it needed to touch every surface. I thought of it as 'the loneliness' not 'my loneliness', because I did not want to keep it. Maybe it was because I was in a town that seemed increasingly to be full of couples and families and tight-knit groups. It was a longing for intimacy that felt uncomfortable and exposing, and that I wanted to deny.

In spite of my good intentions and my work commitments and the new and old friends with whom I tried to fill my time I felt separate and dislocated and started to withdraw. Because what I also felt was shame, which might be the most isolating feeling of all. Why does loneliness feel shameful, when it's such a unifying human experience? We all know how it feels to be lonely. Locked within our individual consciousness, aloneness is fundamental. And contentment in solitude is a beautiful thing, but it's rarely a constant state. When it shifts towards loneliness there emerges something within it that suggests a desire to no longer be alone, a tentative and vulnerable wish for connection, a need to be made real by the accepting gaze of someone else. I worried it poured out of me like vapour.

Of course, loneliness is not something one only feels when alone. There are many different kinds: the loneliness of not knowing what to do next; the loneliness of being in a relation-ship that is no longer right; the loneliness of losing someone you didn't want to lose; the loneliness of pleasing others when it goes against yourself; the loneliness of not being able to protect someone you love from pain; the loneliness of being in pain; the loneliness of not speaking the truth of yourself to yourself; the loneliness of doing the same thing again and again and expecting a different result; the loneliness of fear; the loneliness of addiction; the loneliness of grief.

Loneliness may not make a good story, if a good story is supposed to be full of dynamism and action, but it makes a true story. In Margate, my loneliness met its match in the hard line of the horizon, which some days was wiped away by diffuse mists, or thick clouds that poured into the water like cream. It could stay like that for hours or change in minutes, and my emotional weather was just as fickle, and seemed unnervingly dependent on the skies. There was a loneliness to that too, being so changeable and at the mercy of the elements. It gave me a feeling of unsteadiness, as if I couldn't trust myself, and I cast around for ways to feel more grounded.

To my irritation, I soon discovered it's true that routine is a useful salve for discontent. I'd always resisted it. I thought it was boring and pedestrian, the opposite of the excitement I was usually chasing, but now, for the first time in my adult life, I fell into a repetitive daily rhythm. At daybreak my neighbour's fucking would wake me as usual, which meant I began each day face to face with my solitude or my loneliness, depending on how I looked at it: either I was a free and independent person finding their way in the world, or a lost soul flailing at the edge of things, trying to get a grip on something solid, while upstairs a couple gripped ecstatically onto one another. Within seconds I would scramble to boil the kettle for a flask of tea, pull on swimsuit, jumper, jacket and jeans, grab a towel and my keys and get out into the open. My morning escape fast became a new superstition: if I made it out before the first round ended then the day would be a success. If I didn't, I might as well go back to bed. I tried to be amused by the stark contrast between how we were living our lives – the shagger and the celibate – but it made me feel dislocated, aware of what I was missing. Put it in a story and it would be painfully unsubtle, but sometimes reality delivers the crudest messages.

No matter how lonely I feel or how grey the skies, the sight of the sea always soothes me, like the face of a reliable old friend. Contrary to the monotony of my new routine, down on the beach no two mornings are the same. At high tide waves lap against the concrete boardwalk as though they have nothing to hide, but drawn back they reveal a whole new landscape: lunar, alien. Sometimes the endless metres of sand are scattered with tangles of rancid-smelling seaweed heaving with flies, or crabs by their hundreds, or a carpet of mussels, a glut of starfish or just a light dusting of delicate shells. I love its inconsistency, its fickle spirit satisfies my longing to escape into surprise. There, the loneliness recedes on the breeze, and I can spend hours walking among the lumps of chalk that litter the beach, luminous as bones, evidence of a secret, buried world shifting underfoot. One that deals in footprints and empty things.

The concrete buffers that restrain the cliffs are covered with bold messages in capital letters that people scrawl using bits of chalk spewed up by the sea, and no matter how deep the shade of my melancholy, I can't take myself too seriously down on the boardwalk where the walls shout things like ETHAN EATS ASS and I GET BITCHES ON ME. I NEEDA JCB. YOU ARE THE SUN! TEMPLE OF DUST they yell, as between the rocks bubbles pop, a rich, sticky, mouth sound. I LIKE IT UP THE SHITTER. ART IS 4 DIX!

My favourite thing about Margate is the Walpole tidal pool. Its four acres are held in by high mossy walls that you still see on the water's surface even when the tide swallows them whole, like scars where the skin becomes silvery and taut. At low tide I pick my way along the slippery boundary wall and try not to fall in while the salty overflow laps at my feet – when the water levels match inside and outside the pool it feels like you're walking on the waves. I look forward to the sight of it as though it's a lover, eager to discover whether it'll be inviting or out of reach – my lover is the North Sea, I'm in it and it's in me. After swimming I stand on the side like a clam without a shell, my skin pink and raw as if the saltwater has peeled another layer right off. The cold is brutal but I can stand it and I feel invincible.

In England, cold sea water has been prescribed as a treatment for a huge array of maladies since the late sixteenth century: the water cure was considered the solution for anything from tumours to fevers to melancholy. By the eighteenth century, highly strung women from genteel homes came to the seaside to settle their nerves with a week's course of daily ice-cold plunges, their doctors certain that the adrenaline rush would shock them out of their so-called hysterical symptoms. Maybe I'm playing doctor after all.

I love how the icy seawater grabs at my warm flesh, sets my limbs alive with pins and needles, my lungs fighting for air. I love how it silences everything but the beating of my blood. To plunge into a freezing wave feels like knocking back a shot or swallowing a pill, an act of abandon to the power of something else, something vast and enveloping and out of my control. Sweet relief from the loneliness of my own subjectivity – oblivion can feel so good. (*It was so sweet in my oblivion,* writes the English poet Stevie Smith, who understood.)

This sweetness spills over into what follows – after swimming in cold water your body temperature continues to fall even though you're safely in the warm, and once home I wait for the afterdrop to hit like an addict waiting for a high. It comes on like exhaustion and sweet opiated sleep, and it's a reliable spell against the ghosts of guilt and worry about my father that continue to haunt me every day. I ignore the fact that I'm knocking myself out to avoid my feelings, something I know it's never wise for a recovering person to do.

Before long I started to meet with other people who also liked to swim at daybreak, and my loneliness eased a little. *Dip this morning?* someone would message the group and we'd assemble at the pool, our heaped towels like giant barnacles clustered on the side. It felt good to share the thrill, a flask of something hot to drink, and to make sure none of us stayed in too long. Oblivion felt less tempting in a group.

Eventually, one damp grey night, I also met my upstairs neighbour. He was a man named Dave and skinnier than I'd imagined from the grunts and thrusts that daily reached me through the ceiling. There was a leak coming from his flat and when eventually he answered my knock he appeared in boxer shorts and a thick haze of weed smoke, sinewy, his head shaved close to the skin, his eyes like pins in puffy raw silk. Between his legs an ageing bulldog shuffled into view. I've been having a messy bath, he said, rubbing a palm over his bare scalp as if to wake himself up. Let's leave our landlords out of it, yeah? There was a question mark in his voice but we both knew it was a statement. If you like, I said as he swiftly closed the door, and I was left wondering just how messy a bath could be.

Sometimes threadbare people with jumpy eyes would ring my bell and ask for Dave. I knew he sold the weed he smoked but wondered if he also dealt in other types of drugs. There were several different powders that might explain his frenzied dawn ritual and the urgency of these visitors who came at odd times of the night, looking for oblivion. For now, I found mine in the tidal pool, but I knew it could just as well have come via a bottle or a little plastic baggie.

Here on the coast, was I looking for oblivion or convalescence? At the edge of things I felt a sense, as Eliot did, of throbbing between two lives. Somewhere between illness and wellness, between denial and liberation. The waves are a rhythm where addiction is chaos, but I was supposedly long out of the chaos and I was frustrated to still feel unmoored. Maybe that's why I was drawn to the waterfront for a sense of renewal – the regularity of tidal ebbs and flows was a comfort. And it offered respite from the city: striated dawns, electric dusks, the gentle *slap slap slap* on the shoreline.

Margate's coat of arms has a motto that reads *Porta Maris Portus Salutis*, meaning, 'a gate of the sea and a haven of health'. For generations people have passed through in search of something – the benefits of a coastal life: better skin, better air, better perspective. Maybe even redemption. What does it actually mean, to redeem yourself, anyway? Redemption suggests an exchange – drunk for sober, absent for present, reckless for responsible – but the process of recovery is ongoing. AA teaches that you are forever in recovery, never recovered, that it's a choice you have to keep making day by day. And what about redemption as salvation from sin, error or evil? I don't believe in sin, and addiction isn't a moral affliction. There's nothing inherently redemptive about sobering up. But even if stories about recovery aren't stories about redemption, they are always stories about hope. It's hopeful to hear that the choice to stop can become a possibility, and that it's possible to stay stopped through immensely difficult things.

I knew this, but by the time I got to Margate I'd stopped going to meetings. It happened slowly, almost without me noticing. My arrival in this new town offered me the chance to reinvent myself as someone who didn't need them anymore and it was too tempting to resist. In my fifth year without a drink, I no longer wanted recovery to be the main story in my life. I wanted to start again as if none of it had ever happened, and to forget about the anxious tension in my body, the neighbour who watched me, my dying father. I wanted the optimistic energy of the seaside to help me recover the parts of myself that were light and open to the world.

But above the motto on the Margate coat of arms is a white stallion and a lion-boat, and sitting on top watching over them all – guarding the gate of the sea, guarding the haven of health – is a beast that is half sea monster, half horse. A hybrid creature that never forgets: a hippocampus.

The sadness I'm trying to ignore starts to show up in unsettling omens. On the boardwalk one morning, I find myself eye to angry eye with a hostile gull trying to chew on a rancid chicken breast that hangs from its beak. A few days later, outside my building I discover a little trail of maggots wriggling in a line of stinking ooze that leads from the front door to the Velcro-tipped bin sacks meant to protect against the birds (I look inside and the whole thing is teeming with them, a hundred times worse than the bin in my New York kitchen. I run my tongue over my gums in a reflex and shiver at the memory of those delusional, fevered days). Then, coming home from a party I discover three soiled adult nappies tossed across the tarmac outside my building along with lumps of rotting food waste. It feels like my surroundings are whispering to me about death and decay and some days I am so disturbed, so haunted by it I want to walk right up to a bar and order whatever is strongest, nothing refined, just anything that will numb me out. Or maybe I'm trying to shock myself out of the sadness by toying with an idea I know I won't follow through on – trying to animate myself with the spectre of risk. Instead I go for long walks along the cliffs and when I get home google things like, *how to meditate quick results* and *how to make peace with yourself.*

After a long and violent storm that rages for hours one night in late May I have a particularly difficult phone call with my father. I'm sitting on the floor beside the fake fire, my back to the wall, my left hand absently resting on the blue-painted skull. He keeps asking where I am, then struggles to find enough other words to build the next sentence. He gets caught in a loop where he says a word that's not the one he wants to say, followed by, no, not that, then tries and fails to find another route to the word he intended. He grows more and more frustrated before landing back on the phrase he knows he can manage, and repeats it for a long time, his voice cracking: Where are you? Where are you? Where are you? When eventually I hang up I am frayed and my heart aches. I go for a walk down by the water, hoping it will clear my head.

I find washed up on the beach a bloated seal, dead, its dappled grey skin unmistakeable. The air is heavy and close, the sand manic with clumps of marine litter as though an angry god has trashed it. The creature looks so alone. I watch as a woman with short grey hair dressed entirely in black practises her golf swing at the water's edge, thwacking lumps of chalk with her nine iron into the sea. The tang of smoke carries from a fire somewhere and behind me I can hear children laughing. I reach for my phone but realise with a pang there is no one to tell, so I pick up a wet piece of chalk and scrawl *poor dead seal* on the concrete boardwalk, which doesn't feel like enough. Once home, I light it a candle.

Picking up my green notebook to write a couple of lines about the seal so I won't forget it I flick back through and there, near the start, are the lines about the capers on Stromboli. Reading them I wonder what the philosopher might say to me now. It's good to descend down into yourself – I hear the words in her voice, which sounds like mine, only a little lower – but it's no good if you get stuck there. If so, you're just caught in another trap. And remember, if you close yourself to loss, you also close yourself to love. I don't want to close myself to love, I tell her. I think I want to love more than I want to do anything at all. Well then, she says, you know what you have to do. With a clarity I've been keeping myself too busy to reach, I can see that with my pursuit of the new, with my attempt to outrun my grief, I have still been holding myself at the edge of things, trying to keep things neat, tight with the fear of shattering with more sadness than I can handle. But the sadness has come anyway, and there is no use in trying to deny it.

After that something finally breaks. It seems as if I am always in tears. I cry by the sea, on the sand, in the bath, I cry on the boardwalk and in the kitchen, in the Polish supermarket and on the train. I cry sending emails and I cry silently on the phone. I cry so much that I sometimes laugh while I do it, and think of the scene from *Alice in Wonderland* where she almost drowns in tears. The sadness I've been avoiding crashes over me like a breaker and I stop trying to resist. There's no denying it now, and I understand in my bones that grief is not a shadow you can lose.

It arrives like an engine in my guts, a whirling nauseous tension that makes comfort hard to find. Nothing tastes right, nothing feels right against my skin. Sounds are too loud, nights are too dark and I am tired but don't want to stay still. It's more than that — I can't stop moving. As I walk and walk and walk along the coast I understand that this is my body catching up with what my mind has known for some time, this is my muscles and my organs feeling their way through the knowledge of what we are losing, of what we've already lost, but I never knew grief was such a physical thing, I never knew that it tears through the body like acid. It shouldn't feel like this yet, I think, he's still alive, surely this is meant to come after he dies, and at the back of my mind is the constant thought that I must be doing it all wrong.

No one's company is right, everyone seems fake and too bright and too happy for me to stand. I become vague and snappy with my friends, unreliable. The only place I feel any sense of ease is on the shoreline, where the water and sky are often as restless and moody as me. I move through the days like a wounded animal, trying to apply myself to important tasks, work and logistics, but struggling against the palpable sense of their insignificance. I'm obsessive and my thoughts are relentlessly critical. At night I can't sleep so I comb the internet for answers, and skim endless articles about the five stages of grief. 'Persistent, traumatic grief can cause us to cycle (sometimes quickly) through the stages of grief: denial, anger, bargaining, depression, acceptance', one website tells me. 'These stages are our attempts to process change and protect ourselves while we adapt to a new reality.' They all say that acceptance is the key. I know, I want to scream, I know all about acceptance! I just don't know how to accept this, because this is unacceptable. It's unacceptable to watch someone I love slowly empty out and fade away. I want to refuse, as if in refusing the grief I can refuse the loss, too. But, I realise then, I'm trying to use the water cure for something no ritual can treat. There's a reason we're drawn to the sea when going through something that's too big to fully comprehend – sometimes the only match for oceanic feelings is the ocean itself.

The North Sea has met the force of my sadness with the force of its waves, met the salt of my tears with the salt of its water, met the chill of my loneliness with the chill of its depths. The water held my weight when I carried a heaviness I feared would crush me, and over the months gradually it restored my strength. Now, I am robust enough to go back to the city and face what is to follow. When my lease is up three months from now I know I'll pull the cardboard boxes out from underneath the bed, pack up my things and go home.

After that, gradually, the sadness began to feel more manageable, which meant the loneliness was again able to ebb and flow with greater ease. This in turn allowed for the return of solitude, which came as a great relief. Dawn started to break earlier by the day and I was buoyed by the better weather and the feeling that my decision to go back to London at the end of summer was the right one. I started asking around about rooms to rent, and made sure to start and end each day with my feet in the sea.

The acceptance of grief is an intensely individual path through an uncannily archetypal experience, and there is no single way to do it. It's also not something that happens overnight. Like the tide, the waves came and then the waves drew back, and I stopped trying to fight either part of the process. Soon the beaches heaved with day-trippers and the honey-scented headlands were thick with wildflowers I could name. Jellyfish haunted the tidal pool and friends came from the city to eat pizza on the roof of the harbour arm. The sea glittered gold from morning till night and wild sunsets lit the beach in neon. Under fierce yolk, over misted water, like long-lost pennies back to the sea we go, and at our heels, the anxiety of dusk, dull beneath a Turner sky. I learned that saltwater eats through leather, and a mermaid's purse won't last forever. For a moment, there in that sulphurous stench between blues I was happy, I was happy to the sound of a jet ski, I was happy to the putz of its engine as it died, knowing that soon I'd be home.

Later that June an old friend got married and it was my job to carry her train. We'd been friends since we were ten and there was a long and forgiving history between us – it was Imogen who gave me the kitsch red frame that housed the naked horse-riding woman. It felt good to disappear into a celebration of my old friend's joy, and all the promises of her future.

I did not expect to meet a new future of my own that night but in the ceilidh after dinner that's exactly what happened. I almost sat it out, jaded and tired from my duties, but decided not to resist when two women whose diaphanous floral dresses matched mine pulled me in. The caller's instructions sent us crashing into elbows and stepping on toes, flinging and spinning as we stripped the willow and lost the beat, abandoned ourselves to the sweet oblivion that I always found when I moved my body to music.

In the blur of indiscriminate forms there was one that stood out. My line of three swung round to meet another and I looked up into a smile so broad it made the person wearing it seem like they were made entirely of light. They linked my arm and we did as we were told, spun each other round and landed side by side. Joy radiated off them in waves so strong I felt shy to turn and look at their face. Instead I yelled, promenade, bitches! at the slow couple in front just to detonate my newly nervous energy. Deep laugher burst out of my partner and finally I got a good look at his face: a wide three-cornered grin and big eyes, above which strong brows rose almost to his hairline in amused surprise. He joined my battle cry, then our partners changed again and off he swung into the tent, moving between bodies so light on his feet it was as if he was carried on springs.

If that had been all, I might have forgotten him. Later, when we found one another under a softly lit canopy, I learned his name was J. Over a shared cigarette I listened while he talked as he danced: weightless, elegant, generous. He was a philosophy graduate who made video games that told stories and before the night was over we felt like old friends. Looking back with a romantic's eye, I could say that what I felt then was the start of something important, but at the time we were nothing more than curious strangers and it was simple as the present tense. On the dancefloor Prince filled the night air with his electric falsetto. I moved my bare feet around shards of broken glass and joy flowed between our bodies like reflected light. He took my hand to spin me and I laughed into the warm night, happy to let myself spiral outwards.

The Ouroboros

Death is our friend precisely because it brings us into
absolute and passionate presence with all that is here,
that is natural, that is love. – Rainer Maria Rilke

WE BEGAN A FRIENDSHIP THE old-fashioned way: slowly
and in writing. Twice we met for dinners that stretched
late into the night because of all there was to say. When we
found there was more still we started speaking on the phone.
My spirits lifted whenever the letters of his name lit up the
screen and the new voice in my ear was deep, with a smile
folded into it. He knew I didn't drink and had a father who
was sick but I didn't dwell on those things and it felt good to
define myself differently, no longer a broken thing but a dynamic
one, a person in perpetual motion between the city and the sea.

At the end of the summer I packed up my things and said
goodbye to the waves with a party on the beach. Big beats and

colourful lights on cool midnight sand. It was a farewell and also a hello, a joint birthday celebration with an old friend to greet the next year of our lives. The theme was Sun vs Moon, Chris wore gold and I wore silver, with a headdress made of ribbon and tin foil that I only realised once I finished making it was in the shape of Artemis's crescent. We swam and we danced through the darkest part of the night and by the time I returned to London I felt renewed and determined.

The night I met J. for our third meal in as many months I got ready at my parents' house, which made me feel like a teenage girl. I was excited to see him again, full of a simple optimism that made me think how much less jaded I was now than I had been at sixteen, when good feelings had the uncool shine of immaturity and it was better for your image to broadcast your misery. Nothing was new to me at sixteen, whereas now, at thirty-two, I felt like a novice all the time.

I'd spent the afternoon trying to meet a deadline and listening to the wheeze in my father's chest, worried that it was getting worse. It sounded like there was a rattlesnake inside him that was drowning in mud. All day he'd said nothing but half-sung *I got plenty of nothin', and nothin's plenty for me* on repeat. When he noticed my wet eyes I pretended the tears were from laughter – I'd stopped wearing mascara long ago so I could cry without leaving a trace.

But as I had no intention of crying at dinner I leant into the mirror on the wardrobe door in my childhood bedroom and painted my lashes with Climax Extreme – a big promise, I thought, for such a small plastic tube. Framed by the same square of glass I used at fourteen to daub my lids with army green Dazzle Dust, I observed the face it reflected back at me. It was softened by clusters of thin lines and more strands of white and silver hair spun out at the temples. It felt right that the living I'd done showed on my skin, but the woman who looked back at me understood she'd reached an age where it starts to take a little effort to look like you've made none at all. Above the mirror, an echo of my teenage self still yelled in black sharpie, *I am a pretty piece of flesh.*

I found J. in the queue for a ramen restaurant he'd chosen in the middle of the city. I'd been once before with a friend I slept with when drunk and eventually lost, but they were ghosts I didn't want to summon so I pretended it was my first time there.

It was the kind of warm September night that feels like summer's last gasp – the slow sound of traffic, soft air you want to be out in. Thankfully my nerves were no match for the agile geometry of his face: that quick smile, those brows that danced towards the skies when he talked. The warm resonance in his voice was comfortingly familiar from our hours on the phone but the alert and focused presence of his body was still new to me, and I liked it. His hands were warm, his touch firm but not at all possessive. When I glanced at his face I saw how light pooled in his eyes, the colour of dark honey.

The broth we ordered was rich and smooth and not easy to eat without making a mess. We discovered a shared passion for dumplings, which are a common thing to like but to us it felt like kismet. Dumplings are at the centre of the Venn diagram of my identity, he told me with a grin, the main thing the Polish and the Chinese have in common. We talked and laughed and got soup on ourselves and I was struck again by his humour and his kindness, and that kindness was not something I always used to seek.

After dinner as the sun faded out we walked up and down the river telling each other stories, arms linked, voices overlapping. Walking beside him I felt easy in his company and easy in myself, at home in the city and glad to be back there. I noticed the accounts I gave of myself were different from when I'd dated before: calmer, less performative, more honest. No spin, only what was real. I loved the speed of his thinking and that he teased and took me seriously at the same time. We talked about the city we both grew up in, the people we knew, our past lives and past loves, even those that were unrequited. I was there and nowhere else. What I felt for him then was a radiant curiosity – I wanted to know all there was to know and stay close to the source of his light.

The city admired its own reflection in the river's thick brown water and we lost track of time. When eventually I got home I was struck by the contradiction – I'd got so used to thinking of lost hours as a horror of dementia and involuntary blackouts that I'd forgotten they can also be a sign of something good.

Since coming back for a new beginning in my old city I was renting a room from some friends who lived north of the river, at the top of a tall house with their young daughter (my godchild) and their dog. They absorbed me into their new trio and it felt good to be in the midst of one at the start of things while my own was nearing its end. It was the opposite of my solitary life crying into the sea wind: busy, full of the smell of cooking and the sound of laughter. I no longer wanted to perch on the edge of things, and living there I saw that in my isolation I'd come to take myself far too seriously.

My bedroom window looked out over slate roofs and oddly tropical-seeming trees and in the middle of the night I could hear the neighbours praying loudly through the wall. Sometimes early in the mornings Molly, who was just learning how to talk, would creak open my door and call my name in her small bright voice like a herald announcing me at a party. I was glad to spend time with someone powered by enthusiasm and curiosity, for whom excitement was the main mode of being. Her feelings were big and intense but they changed fast and once gone they left no trace at all. How heavy we become with age, I thought whenever I was around her. How easily weighed down by our beliefs and our regrets and our sadness. Inspired by my goddaughter I resolved to hold onto everything less tightly, including whatever was starting with J.

'Lightly, child, lightly,' writes Aldous Huxley in his novel *Island,* which is about the fragility of utopia. 'You've got to learn to do everything lightly. Think lightly, act lightly, feel lightly. Yes, feel lightly, even though you're feeling deeply. Just lightly let things happen and lightly cope with them.' Huxley was a writer and thinker dedicated to the search for meaning and someone I was willing to listen to, even if here what he says is essentially, get over yourself. Because though I easily found myself bogged down I did want to get over myself, and out from under myself, and – as they say in the rooms of recovery – out of my own way. (It was why I left Margate with few of my things; the furniture I gave to friends, the clothes and books to charity shops, though I hoped to leave more than just objects behind.)

When I was with J., whether in person or on the phone, I felt like I could float above my sadness but also light-headed with nerves. I knew that what went up must come down and worried about where I would land, so I started collecting rules to live by. On my phone was a screengrab of a piece by the American conceptual artist Jenny Holzer, whose bold, text-based work I've always been drawn to. It's a photograph of the Selwyn Theatre in Times Square, New York, which in 1993 displayed the aphorism: *It is in your self-interest to find a way to be very tender.* Like Louise Bourgeois, Holzer has a talent for being direct about complicated things, and her medium is language because she wants people to understand.

In the early days of my recovery, during the hours I spent lying on the blue carpet in Student Psychological Services wishing I were instead floating in the Tyrrhenian Sea, I'd listened to the Buddhist meditation teacher talk a lot about self-compassion. At the time I thought it sounded wishy-washy and indulgent, and with Wormtongue always dripping poison in my ear it had been hard to understand. But now that I knew my sadness about my father had the potential to defensively harden my heart, it was something I was trying to cultivate and I kept the Holzer to hand as a reminder. Somehow I found the message easier to receive when it was delivered like this, not in a gentle voice but shouted into a crowded, heaving metropolis.

Uncertain in myself, I wanted to be told what to do by women artists who get right to the heart of things, so I set the background on my phone to a picture of a neon sign by Tracey Emin, which glowed blue in her handwriting and simply said: *Be Brave.*

For a while I managed to go relatively lightly through my life but then two things happened: my father's condition got worse and I realised I was in love. It was a struggle not to use the pleasure of the latter to escape the pain of the former and I battled the tug of old habits. My father's dementia was now considered 'late stage'. If the loss was once ambiguous it was now catastrophic – too much to get your heart and head around. Words meant less and less and often his mouth struggled to find the shapes of sounds that made any sense at all. Conversation wasn't yet impossible but it was unpredictable and broken by constant misunderstandings. He'd reach for something – a name, a noun – only to hear himself say something else, then find he couldn't retrace his steps back to what he first wanted to say. While I took refuge in the text works of Holzer and Emin that used language to make things make sense, for my father language was now an untrustworthy tool that only made things more confusing. It left him exhausted, and I could see that the language of the body was a better thing for us to rely on. The body will always bring you back to what's real.

Above all I tried to pay attention to what his body was saying. I learned to read it as if it were a text. He never knew if he'd eaten and couldn't always tell if he was hungry but I got to know the physical signs as best I could: a certain slackness in his posture, a glaze over his eyes, or simply the trace of something recently dribbled on his shirt. I observed him closely, struck by the shifting balance between us, aware that long ago he'd attended to my body as I now attended to his, reading it for signs of things that I couldn't yet articulate. After being the object of someone's unwanted attention – the kind that's actually surveillance – practising this kind of tender observation was a great relief, and a reminder that when attention is filled with love it's sacred.

Simone Weil understood attention as opposite to the force of will, which she saw as always trained on an outcome – an achievement, or the sating of a desire – constricting the mind to an unhelpfully narrow and self-centred focus. For Weil, the liberating potential in paying attention comes from a kind of surrender to open curiosity. 'Attention is the rarest and purest form of generosity,' she famously wrote, not because she saw it as a commodity but because she knew that to truly pay attention to someone else you have to first let go of yourself, which can be very hard to do.

It applies to addiction and recovery too. The addict state of mind is a complicated mix of agonising self-focus and a desperate need to escape, which makes sense, considering the paralysing effects of self-absorption. But recovery comes with its own contradictions, because while you try to loosen the grip of this exaggerated sense of self you must also pay attention to the state of your inner addict, and keep it in its place. It's a tricky balancing act, no matter how many years of sobriety you have behind you. Which is why twelve-step programmes teach that the best way to do it is to pay attention to other peoples' needs instead, and avoid the trap of self-focus by making yourself useful to someone else. It's a good tactic, unless this other-focus itself becomes yet another fix.

In any case, when I spent time with my father this was what I tried to do. Mostly I was able to manage it, though I think the idea that I could keep the child in me from searching for the father in him even for a moment was a utopian dream. The important thing was to surrender to the reality of his illness as it was in the present, to what he was like now rather than longing for how he used to be. Painful though it was, as he slipped further towards silence, the impression of the vigorous, alpha man he'd once been softened and was slowly replaced by the quiet, benign presence he'd become. It helped that I'd had to practise letting things go, and it felt good to lean on things I'd learned by being in recovery, to finally put the after-effects of my dysfunction to good use. If I could resist trying to pull at the threads of our old relationship then I could pay real attention to the needs of the person in front of me, who was a person I now knew and did not know, and who knew and did not know me.

At this point he seemed to have almost no memories at all. He appeared to have reached the stage of unencumbered consciousness, but it was hard to tell whether he felt free or whether he felt much at all. If Borges was right about memory making us who we are, if my father was without it, who was it I was helping to look after? It struck me then as a narrow way of looking at things. The end of memory doesn't mean the end of identity so much as a shift in what we understand the self to be and where we locate it. We may be our minds, but, whether healthy or sick, we are also our bodies. A lack of memories doesn't make someone less of a person, and fixating on what's been lost makes it harder to see what remains.

Those quiet autumn days spent living between two families, one old and one new, I found myself thinking often about the shifting role of knowledge in the relationship between parent and child. How ideally the parent knows the child before the child is able to know themselves, and pays attention not only to their every need but also to their coming to consciousness, their becoming who they are. Then, at some point, the parent lets go, and accepts the child as the authority on themselves.

I watched my friends become parents and saw the ways in which it changed them and the ways they stayed the same, and I watched Molly as each day she learned more of the world around her. She would never know her parents as anything other than her parents, no matter how many stories we told her about what they were like before she came along (how wild, how free, how uninterested in a sensible bedtime). It made me wish I'd asked my father more questions about his life while I'd still had the chance.

As for him, he was no longer the authority on himself, not legally, not physically, not emotionally, and he could no longer pay attention to anything much. Even when I was with him I missed him, and I missed who we were to each other, the versions of each of us only our relationship called into being.

Of course, even before he was ill, there were plenty of ways he didn't know me at all, things I kept from him or just left quietly unexpressed. When my spiral into alcoholism was at its worst I hid it from my parents (secrecy is at the heart of active addiction) and once I got sober my father found my use of the word 'alcoholic' to describe myself jarring. Though he was proud of me for stopping doing something that caused me harm, he preferred to take it lightly, saying simply that I didn't drink. At first I thought he was ashamed of me but later I came to see it as a gift – that he wouldn't define me this way meant that in time there would be room for me to find new definitions too.

Our bond had always been an anchor, and the knowledge that it would soon be gone came in and out of focus. Whenever I saw it clearly I felt a deep, old fear of being abandoned.

When I was small I had an insatiable need for my parents' attention, as though without it I would cease to exist. My father worked long days in an office somewhere a universe away and sometimes on another continent, and each morning my mother would close the door to her study and disappear into the *tap tap tap* of her typewriter and the cigarette smoke that snaked out beneath the door. Time works differently for children, for the young mind there are countless eternities in a day. It didn't matter that I was cared for by a nanny I loved and quickly became absorbed in nursery or chasing the cat or playing with a friend, the moment of separation was often interminable agony. One of my earliest memories is of my three-year-old self screaming, arms outstretched over the shoulder of whoever was carrying me, as my parents together walked away from the front door. I remember how the sudden force of my despair heated my body like uranium. There's nothing quite like the white-hot need a child has for love.

What my father needed from me now was quieter than that. Mostly just company while he stared, unfocused, in the silence. Beside him I would hold his hand and do the same, comforted by the softness of his skin, slightly olive and oily like mine, reassuringly supple even in his fragility. His familiar hands with their smooth, flat nails. Hands that used to play the piano and carry heavy bags, turn keys in locks and take those of the people he loved in moments of pleasure. Hold cutlery and steering wheels and glasses of champagne, dial phone numbers, hail taxis, sign papers, wave impatiently, fasten buttons. These hands that could now do very little at all.

Whenever my mind wandered into the past, conjuring old versions of us both, I tried to remember the mynah birds from Huxley's novel that fly around the island of Pala calling *attention, attention, attention*, reminding everyone that the answer to most problems is to be here now.

The trouble is, it's hard to keep your mind from wandering when you're at the beginning of a new love. The philosopher Roland Barthes (side parting, cigarette resting on full lower lip) had a lot to say about it. In *A Lover's Discourse* he breaks down the experience of loving – of being a lover and a beloved – into fragments, beginning with '*s'abîmer* / to be engulfed', which has always seemed to me like the right place to start. My past loves were driven by this kind of overwhelming feeling, especially at first, and for a long time I thought the only type of romantic love worth having was intense and all-consuming. I can see now it's why as much as I was excited about what was developing between me and J., it also made me nervous. I knew how to be sober but I wasn't yet sure I wouldn't lose myself to love. And now I didn't want to drown or get completely lost, though my fear was that I would. That being in love would wake the spiral woman and her insatiable desire to escape.

Addicts, I remember the psychiatrist saying during one of our sessions, while looking me pointedly in the eye, mistake intensity for intimacy. And you know what they say about intimacy? he asked. Probably not, I said, feeling my defences rising. 'In-to-me-see.' He said it slowly, giving each syllable equal weight. It was the kind of patronising baby-talk I'd grown used to in recovery, and which he knew I hated. The pursuit of intensity alone, he continued in his patient and mild tone, is a way of avoiding being really seen for who you are, faults, imperfections and all. At the time I rolled my eyes, but all these years later it still gives me pause for thought. If I saw the times I pushed myself to the limit as rooted in a misdirected longing for connection rather than as total disregard for my life they were easier to understand. As was my resistance to the mundane, which, by definition, isn't intense at all.

I've even found it in writing this book. It's easier to describe the moments of intensity. As soon as they happened, they crystallised into vivid scenes that I've revisited in my mind many times in search of an echo of their initial power. It's because they're out of the ordinary that they immediately become a story. And tying something up into a story can make a complex experience deceptively simple, and distance you from the truth of it, which is bound to be less straightforward. If intensity is about the experience in the moment, intimacy is about closeness over time. Intimacy shifts and changes and emerges in the mundane. It's less exciting to describe and harder to pin down.

At some point in the first two years of my recovery someone gave me a book about addiction and love. It was peppered with line-drawn illustrations like a GCSE textbook and although at the time I found what it had to say about relationships irritating it's another thing that has stuck with me, along with a vivid memory: I'm sitting on the floor in my old flat with Billie, a friend with whom I started a conversation when we were sixteen that still hasn't stopped. We're looking at a double-page spread in this book that's been dog-eared by its previous owner, who underlined much of it emphatically in blue biro. It shows a sequence of drawings of two different scenarios where a cartoon man and woman get together, one on each page. The couple on the left first see each other from a distance, and their gaze of mutual admiration is followed by a drawing of a trumpet and drum vibrating in mid-air − ta-daa, desire! − and immediately they've lost their heads to love. Next, they're in a tight embrace, their kissing faces framed in a heart. After that they stand apart but facing each other in conversation, looking confused. Then in the next image there's even more space between them and they start to turn away from each other. Finally, their backs are

turned completely and they walk apart, the end of their relationship symbolised by a broken heart.

The couple on the right do things differently. They notice
each other but move together slowly, in a series of drawings that
illustrate a gentle progression towards one another. They have
props in their hands to show they have interests other than love
– a tennis racket and an artist's palette. They talk, then they
touch, then they face each other inside a heart. In the last few
drawings they walk, talk and argue, but they stay together.

This is very heteronormative, I say, closing the book. And
old fashioned. And maybe sexist as well. Well OK, says Billie,
who is very patient. But also don't you think there might be
something in it? I did, which was exactly why it touched a
nerve. I knew how it felt to be the couple on the left, those
intense highs and lows. It was powerful to see the kind of love
we borrow French words like *amour fou* and *coup de foudre* to
describe illustrated like that. The same kind of love people sing
and make films about, the kind that's an electric experience
precisely because it's not grounded in reality at all. I realised
the only relationships I'd started like the couple on the right
were friendships.

Those illustrations were on my mind when I went round to
J.'s for dinner, surprised to find myself so full of nerves I almost
called it off. The gentle pace of what was unfolding between us
was a relief because it meant I kept my head but also an anxiety
because it left both of us plenty of space to change our minds.

The thing I used to like about hurling myself into love was
that the glitter of adrenaline blinds you to even your most

substantial doubt. So the song goes: *Fools rush in, where wise men never go*. Before getting sober I was a proud and defiant fool where love was concerned. Rushing in isn't necessarily a bad thing – it's heady and thrilling, and loving is at some point unavoidably an optimistic act of faith – but when the rush wears off you can find yourself tangled up in someone you barely even know, or with little of yourself left to salvage. I had already unravelled once, and after all the effort I put into rebuilding myself I didn't want it to happen again.

But, the song continues, *wise men never fall in love, so how are they to know?* I used to believe that for romantic love to count it had to be a suspension of wisdom in favour of passion, but looking after my father had shown me the importance of really paying attention, which is something it's very hard to do if you rush. I was ready for something different, and I no longer saw passion and wisdom as opposing forces, but understood that they might be even stronger if they're allowed to work together.

As I climbed the concrete stairs to J.'s third-floor flat I realised in a panic that I couldn't picture his face. The sense I had of him was still abstract, a dynamic warmth instead of anything concrete like the specific ratio of his features. What if I didn't like the look of them anymore? When he opened the door with a smile it was a relief to find that I did.

Among the ingredients spread out across the kitchen worktop I noticed a packet of raw prawns without shells. They looked exposed, which was how I felt, sitting up on a high stool, watching as he chopped the chillies that popped red against the green of his close-fitting T-shirt. He must have known it suited him. I took pleasure in the sight of him and the thought that we might be at the start of something good.

When in the sitting room I discovered his wall of philosophy books I laughed out loud. That's a lot of books about truth, I said, pulling out one with a teal cover called *The Philosophy of Time* because it was my favourite colour. Have you read them all? Most of them, he said, when I was an undergraduate, many under duress. I opened the book in my hand at the first page and read:

Consider three fundamental beliefs we have about the world (so fundamental that we would rarely, if ever, articulate them): that change is going on constantly, that changes are caused, and that there are constraints on what changes are possible.

It was good to be reminded that life is change while standing in front of so many books by (mostly) dead and (mostly) important men. Still, I didn't want the metaphysics of causation to spoil the mood so I put the book back on the shelf.

That night in his bed I discovered with J. it was easy to stay in my body. That with him I was able to find abandon without abandoning myself.

The more I got to know him the more I realised that never before had I known such kindred feeling with a straight man. It somehow went beyond any sense of his maleness or my femaleness, beyond the limits of how we presented to the world and any associated roles or expectations to our raw humanity, simply one consciousness to another. It wasn't just that we had a similar outlook – slowly I understood that we literally saw the world around us in the same way. We noticed the same things and were drawn to the same visual oddities and slippages, the same strange juxtapositions. With this shared sensibility came a feeling of being profoundly understood.

In his company I was happy so of course I found reasons to doubt him. The happiness felt too simple, like I hadn't earned it. We'd each turned towards the other so there had been no agonised longing. As much as I didn't want to be engulfed, I panicked that if I wasn't drowned by my feelings for J. then maybe what I felt wasn't really strong enough. For love to count, didn't it have to hurt? I told myself I wanted the kind that could withstand reality but there were still times when I wanted to use the thrill of tortured romance to escape it. Maybe Wormtongue had been right, I thought. Maybe I am impossible to please after all.

I discovered the biggest difference between us was that J. was not compulsive. He had no interest in oblivion. He enjoyed his life but rarely overdid it, allowed himself pleasure but knew when to stop. He liked it up here in the sunlight, and the void didn't call to him at all. In my eyes this gave him a magical quality that I admired as much as it unnerved me. I'd worked hard to accept that the void would always speak to me in whispers, and I was nervous that if he knew it would put him off. I couldn't see it at the time, perhaps because I simply didn't want to, but what underpinned those feelings was shame. I tried to act lightly with him even though it wasn't always how I felt.

My friends teased me about my new boyfriend and I balked at the word, unable to hold the shape of its sounds in my mouth without a grimace. I realised I'd grown attached to the idea of myself as a conscientious objector to hetero romance culture. It was easier to feel I was living in line with my politics when people had to define me by things other than my relationship to a man, and I didn't want that to change. But after all the time I'd spent going down into myself I knew of my tendency to use ideology as a mask for fear.

Then there was the fact that whenever I looked after my father I always left doubly certain that I should call the whole thing with J. off, as if there wasn't room to hold the sadness of loss and the optimism of a new love at the same time. Looking back, I understand it differently. As my father's frailty grew so did the pain I felt around him and I didn't want to turn what I had with J. into a fix. I felt torn in two directions and had to fight the conclusion that love could wait, that things would be easier if I simply stayed on my own. I wondered what happened to the fearless person I used to think I was. ('No one ever told me that grief felt so like fear', writes C.S. Lewis in *A Grief Observed*.)

And so, once autumn broke and turned the leaves russet on the trees, I started smoking more and more and quickly found I couldn't stop. It was annoying to descend three flights of stairs to get outside where it was always cold and often damp, but pleasure was not the point. I was caught in a vortex of anxiety. Now I felt its possibility, terror at the potential loss of love would grip me and I'd mask my anticipatory mourning with the ritual of rolling a cigarette. I'm no good at it but the fact that the tips of my fingers are obstinately out of my brain's control makes it harder to smoke myself into oblivion than if I had a packet of straights.

Chain-smoking is a good example of how loss is always in desire's shadow – you satisfy the craving with the first cigarette but halfway through smoking it you're already thinking about the next one. Once you get the longed-for thing, desire loses its object and casts around for another. That it will find one is one of life's most certain guarantees – we all have drives that are insatiable. Sometimes what we long for does us good, sometimes it does nothing much at all and other times it does us harm. Another of Jenny Holzer's aphorisms is: *Protect me from what I want.*

I found it hard to admit that what I wanted was J. The stronger my feelings were for him, the bigger my fear. I was astonished at my ability to talk myself out of the relationship, even though I wanted to be in it. I found it hard to talk about my grief but I was practised in talking about love so I bored my friends with my worries and they convinced me not to give up on things. You can break up with him in a year, texted Vicky from Milan, but you have to sit tight till then. No sudden movements! But the ghost of Wormtongue haunted my own voice, certain and convincing: it will never work, get out while you still can, it's just another thing to lose, you will not survive any more loss, it's a risk it's a risk it's a risk. I knew it was just the manifestation of my fear and the only way through was to accept it. So I smoked and smoked and, in a late-night trance, furtively stood in the kitchen and ate thick globs of Nutella from a spoon without tasting it at all.

Maybe that's why to soothe my nerves I went often to the dilapidated graveyard nearby. Abney Park is old and huge and overgrown and I found solace in its cool air and the dappled green light cast by ancient trees on stony paths. Early in the mornings I'd be alone save for a few dog walkers and the usual handful of street drinkers still up from the night before. Later in the day it offered shelter to men cruising for hook-ups behind crumbling tombs or in between the mossy headstones. I liked its liminality, how easy it was to get lost in. I felt at home on the bridge it built between life and death, between mourning and desire.

Picking my way through the tangles of undergrowth and fallen branches turning to mulch, no matter how disorientated I got, no matter that over 200,000 people are buried there, eventually I always ended up in front of one particular tomb. It's on a slight incline and has long been smashed open, as if one moonless night its inhabitants tore their way out. Ivy and weeds have reclaimed the collapsed slabs of grey stone, on which are engraved the names Lancelot and Rose Wild.

One day before the sun had been up long enough to warm the air I again found myself standing in front of it, holding the collar of my jacket closed at my throat against the chill, remembering that Freud said there's no such thing as coincidence. I considered the chivalric knight and the untamed bloom, and lit the cigarette I'd rolled before leaving the house. I enjoyed the tiny head rush and tingling in my hands as the nicotine was absorbed into my blood. What captivated me about the broken tomb was its combination of wildness and the attempt to contain it. The boundlessness of life, and love, and death. The ravages of time and the futility of our attempts to stand against them. What drew me to it day after day was my fear that being in love again was reanimating a part of myself I liked to believe I had buried – my compulsive smoking signified the return of the addictive drive, dormant but never gone forever.

So far, my years in recovery had been about learning balance. How to be tender with the wild parts of myself but not let them dominate, and how to separate these drives for intensity and abandon out from the drives of the addict, whose ultimate goal was – as the psychiatrist had so often reminded me – intoxication or death. But balance is a practice, a shifting aim as opposed to a fixed state. If you spend a long time standing on one leg you'll find you have to make many small adjustments to stop yourself from falling. And sometimes you will fall, and that's OK.

If you've been harmed by time spent ruled by chaos it's natural to fear it, but after the loneliness I felt in Margate I understood that fear of chaos can lead you away from the fullness of life into a state of ascetic deprivation. That was not how I wanted to live. A life braced against chaos is also braced against joy. You cannot love without risk.

Even though I hadn't relapsed into drinking, or any of the other ways I used to abandon myself to risk, it frightened me to feel the tug of compulsion reassert itself. I found that to live at its mercy fed the self-neglect that drives my addict – there's still a part of me that wants to totally opt out. But to think of that part as a zombie dehumanises it, when the best weapon in any arsenal against neglect is loving attention. Besides, it didn't seem very tender to think of it like that, and tenderness was what I was trying to be all about. I finished my cigarette and looked at the broken tomb. What would happen if I treated my fear with compassion instead? What about paying it some attention? When I stopped avoiding it and tuned into the fear that made me want to run away from love, I found that behind its mask, the zombie was really just a frightened child terrified of being abandoned.

Days later in the warm dark of J.'s bedroom I finally let it all out. We slipped into some innocuous conversation about the future and I liked it but also felt like I couldn't breathe. The future freaks me out, I told him. It holds this hugely sad thing and sometimes I don't know how to be happy and sad like this at the same time. My throat tightened and swallowed my voice. There was no pretending to go lightly anymore. Tears came with the mass of something heavy and dark. I miss him, I whispered. It was simple, true. It was all there was to say. J. wrapped his arms around me. Say it again, he told me. Say it as many times as you need to.

In the spring I took J. home to meet my parents. I hadn't planned to introduce them so soon but after my father had another particularly dramatic seizure my friends encouraged me not to wait any longer. Who cares if it doesn't work out with J., said Anna Jean, the same friend who had suggested I record my father's voice and who was bolder than me when it came to love. If it does and he dies and you missed the chance to introduce them I know how much it will haunt you. I was conflicted about it, afraid the visceral reality of Alzheimer's might overwhelm J., and feeling protective of my father. But Anna Jean's words were a reminder that I was now in the place where you do things so as not to regret not doing them later, and I knew in my heart she was right.

One cool day in May when the sky couldn't quite decide whether it wanted to rain I brushed my hair, put on a green skirt I knew my mother would like and took J. to the house I grew up in. He coughs a lot, I told him on the way. Sometimes it seems like he's choking but it's just because his oesophageal reflex has stopped working properly. He goes red and it's pretty awful but it looks worse than it is and you just have to wait it out. J. squeezed my hand and I realised I should have been the one reassuring him, but it had been weeks since I heard my father say more than three words in a row and I was lost in anxious anticipation as we waited for someone to answer the door.

My father was dozing in his usual spot, beside a bowl of cherries and a vase of bright flowers from the garden. I poured everyone some tea and listened to the conversation flow between my mother and J., relieved that they both seemed to be enjoying it. Everyone smiled encouragingly at everyone else and I was reminded that when people really want to get on, they usually do. I sat beside my father, who smiled but said nothing, just used his fingers to gently comb through the knots in my hair. When the others went outside for a smoke I asked what he was thinking about but didn't expect him to respond. You, he said simply. What about me? I asked in surprise, and, as if delivering a full sentence were the most natural thing in the world, he answered: How nice it would be to have a son-in-law like that.

These moments of lucidity are one of the most brutal things about dementia. As the disease advances and yet more is lost you keep adjusting to the new normal, and in a process where there's very little comfort to be found at all, linear progression is at least something that makes sense. Then a hole gets blown in the path mapped out from wellness to illness by a minute or an hour or even a day where the old cognition comes back into focus and a simple sentence – *how nice it would be to have a son-in-law like that* – upturns everything you think you know about the experience of the person you love. For months my father had lived only in the now, barely registering any new people he met and only answering yes and no to basic questions like, are you hungry? are you cold? does it hurt? shall I read to you? He was seemingly unable to convey original thoughts, or think outside the present tense at all.

Then, like a conjuring spell, those thirteen words brought back the man who was capable of reflection, whose understanding stretched beyond the moment and his own physical experience of the world not only into his own possible future but the possible futures of other people, including someone he'd just met. As he spoke his face was animated by the spirit I used to know so well – alert, curious, playful – and I was overcome by vertigo at the thought that this version had still been there all along and I just hadn't been doing the right things to find it.

Well then, I said, trying to conceal my astonishment. I'll try my best not to fuck it up.

Though my first love and I had for a minute talked of marriage, it's not something I've ever really wanted for myself. It only appealed to me then because we were young enough that it would have felt transgressive, which was what interested me most at the time – the drama of the idea fed into the intensity I was chasing. As I got older I could never manage to disentangle the idea of marriage from the weight of its history as a binding contract that reinforced the gender binary and was designed to keep women in their place. Because I had plenty of straight and queer friends who felt able to redefine it (and some who didn't want to) I wondered often if it was a failure of my own imagination. Maybe it was partly because my parents' long and complex marriage – which was the marriage I knew best – had been fairly traditional. Watching it stretch into the new shape necessary to make room for the illness that landed inside it I found a deeper respect for the act of making a public declaration of the promise to love another person for a very long time, in sickness and in health, but still I struggled to see how I could become or relate to a wife or a husband without opening the door to the ghosts of every traditional expectation that haunted those words. And they were expectations I had put a lot of energy into rebelling against.

My dad likes you, I told J. when later we were alone in the kitchen doing the washing up. Really? He looked surprised. I'm relieved, I couldn't tell if he even knew what I was doing there. He actually said – I plunged my hands into the hot soapy water – how nice it would be to have a son-in-law like you. Which is not me saying anything about anything, I added, I don't even want to get married, to you or to anyone, I just thought you'd like to know because it's the most coherent thing he's said in a really long time and – I looked up to find his expression was one of gentle amusement. He put his arms around me and I felt the familiar heat of a blush in my cheeks, the kind that comes when you realise you've been caught chasing your own tail.

Seeing my father and J. together made me realise I'd got it all wrong. That I was trying to control things that were out of my hands, or put myself at the centre of something infinite, which is impossible because there's no middle in eternity. My father's surprising moment of lucidity showed me I'd been thinking in straight lines when it was better to try thinking in circles. The beginning of a new love and the end a long life were not things to keep separate because they were already connected, already part of the same limitless cycle: to love is to welcome the spectre of loss, to grieve is to summon the spirit of love.

The ouroboros is an ancient symbol of a snake or a dragon with its tail in its mouth, curled round into an unbroken circle. I used to think of it as an emblem of the kind of solipsism I wanted release from – the self-eating reptile, suspended in mindless pursuit of itself and locked into an eternally dissatisfied cycle, an illustration of how it feels to be trapped in addiction. In fact, its origins are much more expansive and its meaning isn't negative at all. It first appeared in thirteenth-century Egypt as a symbol of renewal and regeneration, and was later adopted by the alchemists to stand for eternity and endless return. It's a symbol of infinity which for the Gnostics represented balance and the harmony of opposing forces, similar to the yin and yang of Ancient Chinese philosophy. For Jung, the ouroboros was an archetype representing the integration and assimilation of the shadow.

I stopped trying to keep love and loss apart and allowed what grew between me and J. to be grounded by the weight of what was happening to my father. Once I gave up trying to keep them separate the fear that held me in stasis lessened, and I found that being in love with J. felt less like falling and more like something we wove slowly together, two stitches forward, one stitch back. Occasionally I got lost in it the way you get lost in a good story, but I never lost my head.

How do you write about love without romanticising it? Aside from this moment where the fading patriarch returns from the brink of silent oblivion to grant us his blessing, there's a lot about my relationship with J. around which you could build a good narrative. We were born in the same hospital and grew up ten minutes' walk apart. As children we read in the same library, as teenagers we hung out in the same shopping mall, as young adults we almost went to a handful of the same parties. You could say that some external force prevented us from meeting until we were ready for one another. You could call it fate, or, to use the seductive language of the white witch, you could say that we were twin flames.

But you could also say it was just chance that we never met before, and there's little mystery in two people who went to similar kinds of schools and universities in the same cities having friends in common. The circumstances in which we grew up were very different − J. doesn't come from the same kind of privilege as me − but the paths we were on were likely to cross at some point. The biggest element of chance is that J.'s parents, both newly arrived from Poland and Hong Kong respectively, chose to settle in the same corner of West London where my parents were also building their lives.

If we'd met while I was still drinking, when what I wanted from romance was immediate intoxication, and when J. was more interested in the drama of being held at arm's length, who knows if we'd even have noticed one another. He's often said he thinks the reason that old and irritating adage that love will find you once you stop looking for it still frequently rings true is that if you're not consumed by thinking about what you want − not constricted by your own will − you're more open to the unex-pected. Whatever narratives about romantic love you might have absorbed can't get in the way of the connection that might be unfolding right in front of you.

I certainly wasn't expecting to meet my partner in a ceilidh at an English country wedding in a scene that could have been written by Jane Austen or Richard Curtis. In my heart I was still a radical free spirit who laughed in the face of convention − clearly, I was also still respecting the delicate ecology of my delusions. I've often thought that the fact that we met dancing − which for us both has always been about joyful abandon − meant we weren't trying to be anything other than ourselves. But however you look at it, shaping a romance into a story at all skims over the mess and doubt involved in favour of the electric charge of chemistry and the thrill of desire, which are important and transporting and also usually only half of the story.

Not long after my father identified J. as the son-in-law he'd like to have, I moved into a small studio flat on the third floor of a glass block with purpose-built surfaces that were white and pristine. The sublet was a short walk from J.'s place and meant we could see each other more without moving in together, which neither of us were ready to do just yet. It was on an anonymous corridor of identical doors and had a wall of glass made from windows that fitted so tightly they created an airlock. My father's seizures were getting more frequent and it felt to me like a spaceship or a laboratory where I could contain the uncontainable and when the time came, lock the door and leave it all behind me. I christened it the space pod and felt on the cusp of things, literally and figuratively suspended, and grew so alert to signs of his impending death I started to wonder if in some small and secret way, I wished for it.

Lucky Seven

THE SEVENTH YEAR SOBER

Not everything that is faced can be changed, but nothing can be changed until it is faced.

– James Baldwin

WHEN MY FATHER TOOK A dive into a plate of fish pie it was a balmy June night and there were red flowers on the table. My mother and I were filling the silence when he snapped forward and buried his nose in mashed potato. We scrambled to lift him but his body had slipped from his grasp. Curled into a determined C shape, he had no power over it at all.

Can you hear me? I said, panicked, as we gripped his shoulders. The words resounded with an authority I did not feel. Internally all I could think was, *No no no I didn't mean it, I didn't mean it, I'll do anything, just don't die, not yet.* His voice was gone but he managed to nod so I asked if he was in pain. It came out in the same tone you might use to say 'hurry up' or 'not now' – urgent and clipped, tightened by fear. With the shake of his head my heart slowed just a little. No pain was something to hold onto.

We tried again to lift him but his form was heavy with resistance. My terror spoke in certainties that weren't mine to claim: a heart attack, a stroke. This body's too heavy to be alive, said the grim detective in my brain, using words learned from morbid scenes on the small screen, terms like lividity, rigor mortis, time of death. This body is an empty house, this body is a ruin.

We sat beside him and counted his breaths. I got down on the floor to read his face while his forehead rested on the table. The unnatural jut of his tightly clenched jaw turned it into a shard, his mouth elongated and knocked over to one side. He looked like a bad drawing of someone I didn't know. For a moment horror replaced love. A thread of his saliva stretched almost to the ground.

Freud defines the uncanny as 'nothing new or alien, but something which is familiar and old-established in the mind'. The dam holding the barely repressed fear of my father's death burst and again I was ten years old, sitting in a sterile hospital room, waiting to hear if he'd survived. It was not where I wanted to be. I forced myself instead to pay attention to the man in front of me, his empty, glazed-over eyes, his hands that curled inwards into claws. His presence then was animal. His body guided by an intelligence rooted in instinct and process rather than intellect or will. Small shocks pulsed his muscles as he fitted quietly in my mother's arms.

I rang for an ambulance and remembered the hysterics of the Salpêtrière, their forms contorted in muscular spasms, their bodies speaking what their mouths could not say. What are you trying to tell me? I silently asked my father. Is it time? Is it now? After such a big and complicated life do you really die in a fish pie? Then, in what struck me as an extraordinary act of self-revival, he vomited.

The stories we tell about illness often do this, ascribe will when there's probably none at play. A cascade of bile that symbolises the desire to stay alive in a person whose agency you've seen slowly eroded is easier to bear than one that is simply the body's reflex to a heart rate that slows too fast. He's a fighter, we said, consoled by the thought that he was not, in fact, ready to go yet.

Before he was ill, my father said several times that if he lost his marbles I should help him die. He'd watched degenerative illness take two of his siblings with its cruel and unstoppable progression and he had a horror of being incapacitated. He could not bear the idea of being a burden. At first I didn't take him seriously – it's one of those things people sometimes say to show their commitment to living, or out of bravado against death – but when it kept coming up I wondered how much he really meant it. I wondered, too, if it was something I could actually do. I'd go to prison, you know, I once said in response, which he conceded was not ideal.

Those conversations replayed in my mind as his seizures got more severe. After each one a little less of him came back. We got to know the local teams of paramedics who arrived in their tidy green uniforms like reinforcements on the front line of a war where my mother and I were tired lieutenants suddenly out of our depth. Always they were patient and capable, but reassuring as they were, there was rarely more they could do than monitor his vitals and wait with us as he slowly came back to life. They usually wanted to take him into hospital and we usually felt he was better off at home. My mother and I, reluctant philosophers, engaged in an ongoing discourse about quality versus length of life.

How do you decide what makes a life worth living? And when that life isn't even yours? At this stage in his illness my father, though hugely changed, seemed largely content. We spoke often in my family of how lucky we were that he had not got stuck in a loop of anger or distress, as can happen with dementia, but now continued to lean back into a benign and watchful state, still largely trusting, still quick to smile, still recognisable to us as the man we loved. Every time I had to confront these questions I got tangled in the problem of how to separate the will of the body from the will of the mind. When he was well my father had a horror of ending up here, but now that he was here, the life within him simply wanted to live. His body possessed a profound will to survive, which I eventually took to mean so did he.

I thought, too, about that terror of becoming a burden to others that so many of us share. It seems rooted in a denial of all that we are – mortal, fragile creatures all destined, if we live long enough, to one day need again to rely totally on others, just as we did in our first tender years of life. There are plenty of cultures that understand this truth and build themselves around it, but not the one I was born into. Mine is obsessed with youth and productivity and denies the existence of old age and illness, even shames people for them. My culture is not one that makes space for the vulnerable. It treats the elderly and infirm like the return of the repressed.

We got used to living in a state of emergency. Each day had catastrophic potential and I woke most mornings thinking, will it be now? Everything else – work, pleasure – felt small and insignificant. I fared better in the moments of crisis than the times in between, where the waiting felt deadlier than anything. Adrenaline and cortisol were reliable old friends from when my life ran on chaos and when they flooded my blood I felt a hit of the familiar intensity.

I became interested in the idea of regeneration. In the space pod one anxious night while J. slept beside me, instead of in his arms I sought solace in the uncaring glare of my phone. 'Does The Human Body Really Replace Itself Every 7 Years?' asked the article on my screen and eagerly I scrolled down to find the answer (it doesn't). But I could see the appeal: if our cells replace themselves in seven-year cycles you can become a new person without even trying.

Soon I would be thirty-three, which meant it was almost seven years since I had my last drink, and, when I really thought about it, seven years since the earliest signs that my father was starting to change. Were we both new people now? One of us changed on purpose, one of us against their will. We were different, that was certain, but I didn't think either of us were new. Nor, I realised, would I want us to be.

But to my tired and wrung-out mind, seven seemed a promising number. I liked the way it looked, with its jaunty lean, like an arrow pointing to the future. It's got a reputation for good luck which I also liked the sound of, and I was ready to be blessed by its sacred symbology.

You find it everywhere, across religions and mythologies, quietly establishing its allegorical dominance: in Christianity there are seven days of creation, seven deadly sins and seven virtues, seven layers of purgatory; in the Talmud and the Quran there are seven heavens; and Buddhism teaches the Seven Factors of Awakening (Mindfulness, Investigation, Energy, Joy, Relaxation, Concentration, Equanimity). In ancient Egypt there were seven heavenly cows and seven paths to heaven, the ancient world had seven wonders. On Earth there are seven seas and seven continents, the phases of the moon last approximately seven days, which in many languages take their names from those of the seven classical planets.

For the Pythagoreans, seven stood for the union of the physical (number four) with the spiritual (number three), giving it unique mystical properties. Although it's been argued that indigo is really just another shade of blue, there are seven colours in the rainbow because Isaac Newton was into numerology and he liked that seven was a symbol of completion and perfection. Indivisible, a solid point of arrival in the scale up towards ten. I looked at J. sleeping beside me and thought, seven plus one.

By the seventh month of 2019, no matter how hard I faced the fact that my father was dying there was nothing about it I could change. Most days it was more truth than I could bear but I was wary of the false comfort of denial so I forced myself to stare it down. He is dying, I said out loud when people asked how he was. He is dying, I said to myself in the dark.

It's easier to understand the kind of dying that's contained and immediate. For most, the ongoingness of a drawn-out death is a horror too far. He is dying slowly, I amended, and watched people back away from me at social events, forgetting you're not meant to answer truthfully when asked how you are. I wondered if I should print myself a T-shirt: FYI I don't drink and my father is dying slowly so you won't find small talk here.

I knew his dying was speeding up when I started to see parts of his face and body in those of people I passed in the city – an elderly man with his mouth on the number twenty-nine, a busker with his eyes at Green Park, a businessman who'd dressed his hands in starched cuffs sitting across from me on the Tube. As if he were slowly disintegrating into the fabric of reality and being redistributed across the features of strangers.

At first it made me angry and I wanted to snatch the pieces of him back. The words *that's not yours* swelled in my throat, accompanied by a physical impulse to grab that I hadn't felt since childhood. So much of grieving feels primitive like that. It collapsed the space between my adult identity and the time when I wasn't expected to hide my overwhelming emotions. Often that summer I wanted to scream until I threw up, or tear my clothes off in fury like when I was two years old. It is reasonable to have primitive emotions, said my therapist.

Instead, I tried to see these apparitions as messages from the parts of my father that were already lost – *See, I'm still here, in the place I'll always be even when I'm completely gone.* I imagined how someone else might find traces of their loved one in my face, too, and found it a comfort. It is surprising what you can get used to.

People talked to me of the intensity of grief but as a simple noun it sounded swift and final, like a strong wind that eventually passes through. Something you could experience and then maybe leave behind. It gets better over time, they said. But grieving was a thing I did in the present continuous, the tense you use for actions that are happening now. It was happening over time and not getting any better. The intensity of it stretched across time and distorted it so much that I could hardly remember a life not accompanied by its beat, but still I was nervous to experience its different form, the kind that's a response to the abrupt finality of death. What if it's worse than this? I said to Billie late one night on the phone. Why do you think it will be worse? she replied.

That August, when death felt very close, I had flashbacks to my drinking days. It unnerved me – they were common in early recovery as I tried to understand what happened, but after this long they felt less like memories than scenes from someone else's life. Falls, cuts, fights – flashes that appeared, vivid and intrusive, while I sat on the bus or did the washing up, or waited in line at the doctor's. I noticed they came most often when I was doing something mundane, like a rebellious taunt: come back, come back, maybe this pain is better than that pain after all. Never the good bits, but things my body had been through while my mind was absent from it, or at least distorted. Impressions in skin and bone. They came in partial shots from odd angles or with the sense of a dull ache and a distant muscular pain. Hauntings from another dimension.

They were a caution against complacency, an urgent message from my unconscious: it wouldn't take much to send you back here, to the place where everything hurts. But they also felt like a whisper from the void: it wouldn't take much to bring you back here, away from the place where everything hurts. Take your foot off the gas and let go.

Or maybe it was because my father now moved like a drunk. My job was to catch his body as it fell – out of nowhere he'd forget how to use his legs and they'd buckle. It began when, walking up the garden steps one morning, he found himself stuck, the connection between his brain and his limbs momentarily severed. I don't know how, he said, looking at his feet in confusion. With one of his arms slung around my shoulders I reached under his left knee to lift up his left leg, then his right, then his left again, and in this way we swayed towards the house inch by inch like a strange two-headed crab.

His skin became a map of yellowing bruises that surprised him throughout the day. He had no idea where they came from. Sometimes I'd catch him examining the marks on his shins or forearms with anxious curiosity and it always struck me how much time had passed since I'd had to decipher the mysteries of my own body that way. It reminded me I was lucky to still have the use of it at all, and sometimes it's wise to feel lucky – it can train your mind to notice what's good.

When my birthday came around we decided to celebrate with a nice lunch and do our best to ignore the fear that it might be the last one we'd share as a family. The restaurant was quiet and comfortable, a smart place near my parents' house with tasteful grey walls and plush velvet seats that moved soundlessly across the carpet when pulled back. Starched napkins and emphatically discreet staff. It was the three of us plus J. and a couple of old friends, and we dressed my father in elegant clothes and sat him at the head of the table. He looked like he was mostly somewhere else and I was reminded of the teddy bear's picnics I used to stage as a child, my favourite toys arranged like guests, propped up on chairs, their glass eyes fixed on nothing while I talked as if they could hear me. When a waiter placed an amuse-bouche in the shape of a miniature plant pot full of miniature carrots that you were supposed to eat with a miniature spade in front of each of us I burst out laughing and almost looked around for the Mad Hatter, thinking, we're really through the looking-glass now.

My father fell asleep and I battled a heavy feeling of futility. The food was good though I remember none of it apart from the dessert, which is when things became eventful. The arrival of a delicate and convincing green pudding shaped to look like a real pear and an elaborate cheese trolley on silent wheels signalled a descent into terrible farce.

Cue the music, dim the lights.

This Reblochon is very special, the cheese man said with a flourish, creamy and strong. And this, he pointed to a slab of something hard and yellow, is our award-winning Comté. I glanced over at my father to see his head had dropped onto his chest. The pear pudding glistened and shivered in the middle of the table. Meanwhile, the Mimolette, continued the cheese man, and I saw my father's jaw begin to clench. No no, I said, to the affront of the cheese man, though it wasn't him I was addressing, I was speaking to the knowledge of what was coming next. No no. The orange colour of the Mimolette, continued the cheese man as my father's fingers curled into claws and his transformation into his animal self rolled on, comes from the addition of natural colouring. Something's happening, I said, quietly at first – you don't raise your voice in a place like that – as my father's body started to judder. In my body I knew what was coming but my mind was infuriatingly slow. Something is happening, I said, louder, but everyone else still faced the cheese man, who had much more to say. Something is happening! I shouted, jumping out of my seat, at the same time as the others all caught on. Time went from slow to fast and everything happened at once. I shouted for a bucket and a silver champagne cooler flew towards me through the air just in time to catch his vomit. The waiters cordoned off our table with white cloths and military efficiency and two paramedics appeared as if they'd been waiting in the wings. My mother elegantly handled the other diners and everyone was very kind, the shock on their faces a reminder of the extremes we'd grown used to.

As the paramedics wheeled my father out to the waiting ambulance I took in the table scattered with tumbled things. Everything was in disarray except the pear pudding, which remained perfect and smooth, its glycerine surface troubled only by the reflection of my anxious face.

Six months later I wrote about that day in an article for a magazine. The brief made a complicated thing sound simple: *A piece about a time in your life which brings in a moment of change that means you start to see the time differently, ending on a final resolution.* It was the first time I'd written about my life for such a large audience and while I was nervous of people's judgement I liked the illusion that I could hold something as uncontainable as ongoing loss in sixteen hundred words. In the confident style that befits those publications I told the story of my father's illness and how it related to my recovery. I reflected that both started to happen at the same time and realised that in hindsight I could see my commitment to sobriety was grounded in an unconscious knowledge that, in order to face what was coming without falling apart, I needed to grow up. There was the promise of satisfaction in trying to find a resolution to things I knew to be irresolvable, addiction recovery and dementia – perhaps if I wrote about the resolution I would find it. Some things only start to feel possible once you put them into words.

But it's impossible to contain something at once so colossal and so mundane as death in life and life in death in an article, or even in a whole book.

Outside, the temperature dropped and an autumnal damp settled around the city. Inside the house I grew up in we faced a different kind of chill and a new euphemism worked its way into the family vocabulary. Though I said them plenty to myself and other people we still struggled to say the words 'death', 'dead' and 'dying' to one another. Instead we started to speak of 'last things', an oblique way of naming the suspended reality in which we lived, and the looming prospect that would eventually bring us crudely down to the muddy ground. Ashes to ashes, dust to dust, the crushing weight of the inevitable. My mother and I went out of the house to talk about it – somehow saying those words inside its walls felt like a betrayal. Over fish and chips in a restaurant I'd never been to before and to which I'll never return we tentatively spoke words there's no coming back from, like 'crematorium', 'funeral' and 'eulogy'.

Meanwhile a new horror worked its way into the body of my father. Now when we sat quietly on the sofa, both of us wrapped in colourful shawls against the grey, sometimes a lascivious look crossed his face. His body became possessed by urges disconnected from the sight in front of him, his eyes not deciphering his present reality but time travelling, projecting a new context onto the person before him. At the time I was the age my mother had been when they met and there were days when I looked quite like her, similar enough that it might confuse a mind living in a reality from over thirty years ago. A reality where I did not exist and he was in the first flush of a new love. Or maybe there was no story to it at all, just a misplaced animal urge from a body and mind that now lived outside narrative.

In response I had nightmares about ex-lovers who came to me as monsters in the darkest part of the night. The dreams always ended the same way: at the threshold to the kitchen of my old flat I stand flanked by my mother and my aunt, refusing to let the unwelcome visitors pass. The monster-lovers are disbelieving but we are an impenetrable wall. Though in the dream I was comforted by the presence of the women I love, each time I woke into a feeling of resignation that I must face what was coming next alone.

In banishing the figment lovers in the dream I banished the part of my father I could not bear to see, the part that I did not want to contaminate the man I knew, trusted and loved. I was angry with the disease, but what good is it to be angry with a disease? I had to be angry with something.

Sometimes it was hard not to also banish the real lover from my waking life, who could not have been less monstrous, and who was generous with his love and support. But fixated as I was on the ending I'd feared for so long, it was still hard to allow myself to accept a new beginning, no matter how much I wanted it. Instead there came an impulse to self-sabotage with a practice run – to reach for control by ending a beloved relationship on purpose before another one was ended by something out of my hands. To prove to myself I could survive it. I felt the pressure of my bolting instinct return to my body like an itch on the inside of the skin.

Love reveals its strength when it's tested. Instead of running away, I tried to remember the words of the French philosopher Alain Badiou, who in photographs has a kindly face that gives him a grandfatherly air. He describes love as 'a tenacious adventure', and points out that although we enshrine the thrill of its beginning in endless stories, it's what follows that makes it something profound. Tenacity is just as important as desire if you want to build a love that lasts. And we were building something,

I realised as I woke beside J. on yet another grey morning and finally understood his face had come to look like home.

And so it was that my father and I both found ourselves facing new homes that November. Mine was figurative but his was a literal construction of bricks and mortar as we accepted that what he needed now was round-the-clock care. It's confronting, the knowledge that your own care is not constant enough, that your emotional care – which is round-the-clock, which takes no hours off, even when you're far away – is insufficient if it can't be translated into the tangible labour of caring, for every hour of every day, and also every night. 'Round-the-clock care' is both a description and a euphemism, a way of making something messy into something neat. A way of articulating and then facing the limitations of what you are willing and able to do for someone else.

The nursing home was not far from the house I grew up in. When we learned they had a room we thought, what extraordinary luck. My aunt came over from Australia and arranged for three weeks of respite care so my mother, who was exhausted and becoming ill herself, could have a proper break. We couldn't think of it as more permanent than that and so we didn't try. Just a short stay, we said, as the nurses exchanged knowing looks over the tops of our heads.

The day we took him was cold and bright. We loaded a taxi with blankets and cushions and pictures from home. His room was small and light with French doors that opened onto a peaceful garden. It reminded me of other temporary homes – hotel rooms, hospital rooms, my bedroom in university halls. My orange coat matched the armchair and the bedspread and I was comforted by all the vivid colours, that the place wasn't painted in shades of porridge or old pea soup.

On my twice-weekly visits I would arm my sadness with miniature doughnuts from the bakery by the station (not a patch on the ones from Peter Pan but still good enough to sweeten the deal). We'd eat them together in a silence broken only by the coughing fits that always came after he swallowed, which were getting steadily worse. In each new spluttering round, the spectre of a breathless ending revealed itself. Time stretched on and my father stayed where he was. It was clear to us all that he was safer there, more comfortable, and we gradually came into the knowledge that it was where he would remain. A place better equipped to contain the unravelling of his body, cared for by people better equipped to withstand it, who didn't have to make the dizzying switch between two roles played at once.

As is normal in late-stage Alzheimer's, his oesophageal reflex grew weaker still and the coughing fits got so violent that he was quickly moved to puréed food. I was bereft without the ritual of the doughnuts. Now that he barely spoke at all they felt like the last thing we could share. Instead I would sit beside him in his single bed watching high-saturation shows with no plots to lose track of, *Bargain Hunt* or *A Place in the Sun*, with the heating cranked up to twenty-nine degrees, and the flowers my mother always brought wilting in real time. J. and I are talking about moving in together, I told him, watching his face for clues that he understood. I'm nervous but I think it's a good idea? Eyes fixed on the television, he scratched at his leg, and seemed not to know I was there.

It was a sharp January day when J. and I moved our things into a first-floor rental on a quiet, tree-lined North London street. It was strange to see my possessions mixed together with someone else's after so many years on my own. Outside our bedroom was a terrace, and beyond it, a valley made by our neighbours' gardens, which were long and deep. They had big trees and sheds, soft well-kept lawns and their shrubbery was evergreen – we were temporary residents but most of them were not. There, my feet were still off the ground but closer to it than in the space pod and as we unpacked I gave in to the gravity pulling at my heels. I imagined roots sprouting from the soles of my feet. It was a tentative feeling, full of potential. At the same time I was frightened of getting stuck, but down is not the only direction in which a root can grow.

Rhizome is the botanical term for a creeping rootstalk that runs horizontally underground beneath a plant sending out roots and shoots that can grow in all directions, both down into the soil and up towards the sunlight. I first came across it not in its botanical context but during one of those long nights in the library when I was trying to think about philosophy instead of thinking about love. It was via the work of the clean-shaven post-structuralist Gilles Deleuze, whose extreme side parting and furrowed brow identified him as a very serious intellectual, and his scruffier-looking partner in writing, the psychoanalyst Felix Guattari, whose disorderly curls flew around his face giving him the look of a mad scientist always on the brink of shouting, *Eureka!* In their enormous two-volume work of criticism, *Capitalism and Schizophrenia*, they use the rhizome to describe a mode of thinking and interpreting the world that revels in the ways in which everything is interconnected. There's no hierarchy in a rhizome, no discernible centre, no beginning or ending, just the nodes of different possibilities. It's about flexibility and dynamism, growing towards infinite new connections.

I hadn't thought of it for years but it was on my mind as I surveyed the evidence of this new shared life: J.'s plants, my shoes, the enormous Ikea rug we bought together to cover the chipped laminate floor. In my twenties I thought of roots and the stability they stood for as binding and restrictive – I wanted to chase the new, not see what might grow out of staying put. Then, feeling rootless was the same as feeling free. But the interesting thing about the rhizome is that it represents not restriction but possibility, the potential to flourish in any direction. It gave me a way to think of stability as an opening-up instead of a closing-down. The home I was building with J. didn't have to represent the complete merging of two lives or the creep of a suffocating conventionality but a node of interconnection in a vast, limitless root complex spreading out into the world. Not restriction, but yet another way of feeling free.

At the end of February in 2020, I went to Australia to visit my aunt in what I now look back on as a dream-like interlude before the world was forever changed. For months, I agonised over booking the trip. I'd be gone for two weeks, the longest and furthest I'd travelled since the word 'Alzheimer's' took up its firm residence in my vocabulary. But I also knew that over the long years of my father's illness I'd neglected the other relationships I cherished, and I needed to pay them some attention. I was worried he'd die while I was gone but I was also exhausted and ground down and wanted to fortify myself for what was to come if he didn't. I booked my flights on the shortest day of the year and left the feelings of guilt for my future self to deal with.

By the time I dragged my suitcase across the shiny departure hall floor, a strange word was working its way around the globe, landing in each new language like a UFO: Coronavirus. It was the reason I had a handbag full of antiseptic wipes and hand sanitiser and wore a black mask looped obediently over each ear. So far, England was fine, but the virus was spreading fast through other parts of the globe and airports were even less relaxing places to be than usual. I arrived at Gatwick at breakfast time and stepped into an officious, subdued vacuum, at the start of something far bigger than most of us then knew.

My first stop was in Dubai, where I had a layover of a couple of hours. The strange new bug had been picking up pace in the Arab states and while my flight was in the air more borders had closed. We arrived in the evening, and before my fellow passengers and I could set foot in the airport our temperatures were checked. Two men in traditional Emirati dress manned cameras with thermal screening technology and I filed obediently past, hoping my blood was not too hot, willing my outline to stay blue and grey.

Things were well organised and calm in the new dystopia. Never had I been more aware that airports don't have windows you can open. Everybody wore face coverings and many had the pale blue hands of surgeons because of their latex gloves. I walked past the glass walls of the smoking lounge and watched a man lower his mask to take a drag of his cigarette as the smoke billowed around him. It was an image I'd recall months later when the World Health Organisation issued illustrations that showed the virus as a cloud of airborne infection, like an invisible mist.

Within the terminal was a simulation of a street market with stalls where you could get all sorts of things, dumplings or banh mi or fried chicken or noodles. It felt like a low-budget film set. As I tapped my card to pay for some spring rolls, I tuned into the song that was playing. *Freed from desire, mind and senses purified.* It was one I knew but hadn't heard for a long time. *Freed from desire, mind and senses purified.* I thought of the man in the glass box filled with smoke, and felt glad that for now I was at least freed from the desire for a cigarette. A few months ago I'd quit yet again, and was still full of strident early resolve. *Freed from desire, mind and senses purified*, the song insisted, just like a craving. Was being freed from desire really the answer? I wasn't sure I wanted a purified mind and senses, it sounded very dull. And besides, sometimes desire feels good.

After all the going down into myself to do as Simone said and try to tear desire from its object, I knew the difference between my genuine impulses and the ones that were to do with mindless escape. The freedom I finally found in recovery lay there, in the ability to choose which ones to follow.

As I folded into my window seat on the next leg of my journey, I noticed that above me there were LED lights embedded into the plane's moulded ceiling. The main lights went down for take-off and they revealed themselves like a hidden constellation. Out of the window, I was pleased to see the low-slung moon hanging just above the runway's orange blinkers. It reclined in a lazy backward stretch. Hello Artemis, I thought, and the engines rumbled into action behind me.

When I landed, Sydney was warm and busy and the virus was still a distant news story unfolding a long way away. It was good to breathe different air and be back beside the sea. To snatch a couple of extra weeks of summer while at home it was cold and wet, and spend time with my aunt in the place where she had made her life, where it was easier to talk about things other than the sadness in our midst. The days went by in gentle contentment and reminded me there was another kind of life, one that doesn't lurch only from crisis to crisis. Each morning I promised myself I'd ring the nursing home tomorrow. The tomorrows stacked up and soon there weren't many left before my flight home.

On my last day in Oz I went to swim at a saltwater women's pool cut into the rocks at Coogee. It was a magical place, secluded, with glistening clear water and barnacled walls that looked out over the ocean. Draped on the surrounding rocks were women of all ages enjoying the warmth on their skin and this refuge from the male gaze, with its commodifying impulse, its drive to possess. Though while there I learned that the history of the pool itself contains a different version of the same impulse – before it was colonised by white settlers the land belonged to the Eora Nation, for whom the naturally occurring pool that preceded the concrete one I was there to swim in was a sacred site. As I descended the steps to the water I thought about that drive to take what's not ours, to make possessions of things that should remain free, that is so fundamental to human history. Everyone was clustered in the distant corner of the pool catching the last triangle of sunlight as the burning star slipped slowly behind the hill. Light from the ripples of water reflected onto my thighs and I noticed the thread veins starting to spread across them, tracing small broken paths over the flesh. Then, in an instant, the sun was gone and as the shade swiftly claimed me I wondered, if you cut me in half, how many rings would you see? Would they tell you my age in years or in spirit?

I returned to a shell-shocked city at the beginning of spring and a newly restricted life. We were none of us in Kansas anymore. While I was away J. had bought masks and antiseptic wipes and filled the kitchen cupboards with food that wouldn't go off. I didn't know you were a prepper, I said, still attached to my denial, not yet able to understand. For all my attempts to predict the future, I could never have imagined this. Reality was unrecognisable.

The nursing home closed to visitors. The first lockdown began and with it fear arrived and settled in my chest like a bird building a nest. Over the days that followed I watched all my escape routes disappear. We queued outside the supermarket and tried to understand the numbers on the news. A climbing daily death count, the preparation of a new hospital named after a songbird and a long-dead nurse equipped with 4,000 beds and two large morgues. A wave is coming, the papers said. Brace yourselves, a very big wave is coming. Reality was now authored by George Orwell, everybody said with tight wry smiles, even those who hadn't read his books. Stay well, people told each other, a warning and a threat. The prime minister clenched his plump pink fists on his desk like ripe little hams and told us on all accounts to STAY AT HOME.

Instead of the rhythms of the seasons, we fell into a life dictated by the rhythms of government restrictions. Time collapsed in on itself and there was very little to do. We cooked, we cleaned, we felt guilty that we didn't cook or clean enough. Relentless domesticity was not the life I wanted but the pandemic made *femmes maisons* of us all. The weather was uncommonly good, every day a thick blue sky. In the uncanny stillness of a city asleep I watched the California lilac in the garden next door bloom into a billowing indigo cloud. It was a blue that made me think of other things – the density of a Madrid sky in June, deep sea, suede shoes. We hung out of our windows to clap the NHS. It felt inadequate, emotional, vital, ridiculous. Each time it made me cry. The malaise that settled in my mind and body reminded me of depression and guilt-ridden hungover days. It fidgeted at the mental door I'd worked so hard to keep shut and I was glad to have the buffer of the sober years I had behind me.

Unable to visit my father across the city I spent hours each day on the phone to him. He couldn't say more than a few words at a time so instead of a conversation I described what I could see from my windows – from the front of the flat, two magpies building a nest. From the back, the extravagant lilac, its flowers an electric zing of contrast to the humming green of the valley. What else can you see? he'd ask over and over, just so I'd stay on the line. Each day he heard it all again for the first time, and each day I tried to see it for the first time too. It became our joint meditation.

Work dried up and J. and I watched endless hours of TV. We couldn't live our own lives so we fled into those of gangsters in '90s New Jersey. Now whenever we dropped something in the kitchen we yelled, Ouoh, Madon! and dreamt of gabagool. It didn't take long in confinement for my vegetarianism to lapse.

There's a poem by Ada Limón, 'Love Poem with Apologies for My Appearance', that opens with the line, 'Sometimes, I think you get the worst of me'. I thought of it often then, when I looked over at J. on the sofa. When we moved in together we had no idea our lives would become this small, this reliant on one another. As with the 'I' in the poem, all trace of my outside-world persona fell away, leaving behind a stripped-back, pyjama-clad version, loving but often tearful, absorbed by fear and guilt as she paced the flat for hours at a time clutching a phone to her ear enunciating clearly about the colours of the cars parked outside. Itching for escape beyond that provided by packets of biscuits and the big black rectangle of the television.

Those days trapped inside I was glad of its big screen but I'd never owned a television before, not because I didn't watch things but precisely because I did. I felt powerless against the logic of the streaming mechanism as it cued up the next episode of whatever it was, the reluctant knowledge that I needed to tend to the mundanities of my real life subsumed by the temptation to numb myself instead by escaping for hours into the fictional world of a Chicago law firm or forensic detectives in Miami or a gossipy seaside town populated by people with impossibly symmetrical faces. Not for pleasure or relaxation, but simply to disappear. Somehow if I kept it to the small screen of my laptop the impulse felt more contained. When I looked at the vast, dark, sharp-cornered shape I saw a visual manifestation of the void, fearful that I might tumble into its black expanse, never to come back out.

It was a side of me I was nervous for J. to see, but there was no hiding anything now. And the intimacy that grows out of the unvarnished truth offers its own kind of freedom: 'I move in this house with you,' writes Limón, 'the way I move / in my mind, unencumbered by beauty's cage. / I do like I do in the tall grass, more animal-me / than much else.'

Enough weeks in that we'd stopped counting and half-accepted our limited new lives, one morning my father interrupted my monologue about the magpies and the lilac. In a voice strained from disuse, he whispered, Say. Something. Original. His old impatience was a flare in the dark, proof that the man I missed was still there. My laughter startled the birds.

On my desk was a copy of *The Red Tenda of Bologna*, an essay by John Berger that Carrie had given me which I had not yet read. OK, I said, holding the small volume open with one hand. Let me read you something good. Together my father and I accompanied Berger as he described a beloved uncle who loved Bologna, and whose loss the essay is grieving. The piece unfolded into a meditation on death and loving, and how the finality of the end of a life is not as total as it might at first seem. There are bonds between people that reach beyond death – impressions of loved ones stay vivid in the things they liked and in the memories of those they leave behind. Berger's words transported us beneath Bologna's famous colonnades with their distinctive red awnings (the eponymous *tendas*) and reminded us that there are ways to communicate across the impossibilities of space and time. That in fact we were doing it right now: though physically separated, the essay ensured we were together in those arcades, drinking Blue Mountain coffee from Jamaica, whispering across dimensions in the pilasters, resting our heads on pieces of red linen folded four times. 'It crosses my mind that a *tenda*, as well as being a blind for keeping sunlight out,' writes Berger, 'may also be one for keeping grief in, and for cultivating determination.'

When I reached the end my father simply said, Superb.

In the indistinct time that followed he developed recurring chest infections that meant he was in and out of hospital. There were no visits, and the constant terror of Covid. It was years since he had been able to operate a mobile so if we wanted to talk to him we had to rely on the busy ward phone. Difficult as it was, the change of scene would sometimes open up old pathways in his mind and he'd astonish me by speaking fluently again. They've put me on a ward where there's not much hope, he told me down the crackling line, before drifting into a hallucination where an old colleague was in the bed across from him trying to send a fax. Is it scary? I asked, relieved when he said no, though I wondered whether he was trying to reassure me. I've forgotten the thousand words I had to say to you, he said the next time I rang. I still wonder what they might have been.

On June the 23rd the government announced that in two weeks restrictions would finally start to ease, and for the first time in months I noticed the date: my seventh sobriety anniversary was the following day.

When I began drafting what you're reading now, my plan was to end things here, in 2020, as I sat in soft blossom-scented air under a hot June sun drinking a cup of tea on the terrace. The fact that this anniversary came around in circumstances that meant I barely noticed it seemed a good way to show that freedom isn't always found in a sense of soaring euphoria – sometimes it's most deeply felt in peace. Lucky number seven, with all its completion-related symbolism, would be a satisfying place to end things and I was pleased, too, by the double meaning of 20/20 in a story that is so much about coming to see things clearly. But plans are funny things. Like stories and myths and pieces of writing they're attempts to contain the uncontainable. Sometimes they work out but often enough they're thwarted by the universal chaos inside which we like to imagine we have control over our lives.

Such a neat container would be misleading about the reality of recovery and the reality of loss. There are no tidy endings, only days that follow other days, that stack up into months, then years, and so on. Neither completion nor perfection are useful goals for a person in recovery. A death is not an epilogue, and to make it one would be to let it slip back into the shadow of denial.

From that day, it took just under seven months for my father to catch Coronavirus.

In the time between that peaceful June morning and his positive test result our relationship continued to be conducted by phone and occasionally through panes of glass. When lockdown restrictions were lifted I was allowed to spend one windy hour a week with him under a pop-up gazebo in the nursing home garden. We each had to sit two metres either side of a free-standing sheet of Perspex fixed to walls of orange mesh fencing that stretched all the way across the tent to enforce absolutely no touching. We both wore masks and surgical gloves. I would shout across the distance while he shivered in a wheelchair beneath layers of clothes that never seemed protection enough for his fragile body against the cold. He would drift in and out of consciousness. Occasionally the nurses would wheel him up to the partition and turn a blind eye so I could kneel on the damp ground, douse my gloved hands in astringent sanitiser and reach them through the netting. For a couple of minutes we'd hold awkwardly onto one another while the smell of rubbing alcohol filled our nostrils in the silence. I would search his eyes for some sign he understood that this cruelty was not my choice, that if I could tear down the barriers and take him in my arms then I would.

The cold weather brought more infections and more lockdowns. To minimise our risk of exposure, J. and I got used to walking the two hours it took to cross the empty city in the dark. It was strangely beautiful in the clear air and eerie calm of suspended animation. My determination grew stronger, as did my calf muscles. When gazebo visits were cancelled we stood instead on the pavement in front of the nursing home's bay window, which framed my father as though he were a mannequin in a shop window display. For sale: one tired, confused, genteel bag of bones. Separated by the pane of glass, we spoke to him on one of his carers' phones, pleased that at least without the need to wear masks it was easier to make him laugh.

The week he was due to receive his first vaccine dose, I got the call I'd been dreading since the start of the pandemic. My father was one of several residents testing positive for the virus. *Be Brave*, said my phone when I hung up the call. It was Twelfth Night. Eleven days later, he died.

Before the pandemic turned touch from a comfort into something deadly we last saw each other on one of those winter mornings where everything is muffled beneath dense white clouds. I was about to leave for Australia. Outside it was freezing but in my father's room it was eternal summer. There were yellow roses beside his bed. Usually I'd find him asleep but this time he was dressed and waiting in the armchair, leaning forward with his shirt sleeves rolled up, hands clasped, deep in thought. Hello love, he said, his voice so strong and bright that it tore a hole in the space–time continuum and we travelled to a dimension where his Alzheimer's didn't exist. I sat beside him and held his hands. He wanted to talk about his mortality. I'll be lying there, he said, gesturing across the room, on that bed, until I die. We both looked at it in silence. It was narrow, on wheels, neatly made up. How does it make you feel? I asked. He laughed, two short syllables, and an amused and mildly surprised expression crossed his face. Slowly, he simply said, All right.

I last saw him in January of 2021 as he lay dying in that bed, which was at once twenty minutes and a galaxy away. J. and I were with my mother in the house I grew up in. Her heart was increasingly fragile, which left her at high risk from the virus. If I went to my father's side I would have to isolate from her for the next fourteen days and she would be alone. There was no question as to what I would do, or whether it's what he'd have wanted.

Against the plump white pillow his head was angular and small, framed by the smudged screen of the iPad. He looked light, delicate, like a desiccated flower moments away from crumbling in the wind. My attention was focused by adrenaline and the rest of my surroundings fell away. In the top right corner floated a digital version of two tear-stained faces – my mother's and mine – reflected in miniature, as though we were looking down on him from a great height. We were beamed large on the corresponding screen propped up beside his bed but I wasn't sure he knew. His eyes looked unseeing, lit only by the faintest glow of what used to animate them as it receded further into the distance.

We talked to him. We strung words into sentences to make continuous sounds that might conjure our presence beside him. We told stories, and dug up long forgotten memories, and said the things we imagined it would be good to hear: thank you, I am with you, I love you, you are not alone. Occasionally a disembodied blue hand would reach into the picture and moisten his lips with a water-soaked sponge. As on a film set, out of shot there was a whole invisible production – nurses and carers in disposable bodysuits and gloves, eye goggles and N95 masks, risking infection so they could ease his transition. Tender stand-ins for those of us that loved him.

And so, during the two days and one night it took for his life to end we staged a surreal deathbed scene. I put make-up on to video call my dying father. Absurd though it now sounds I tried to make myself look less stricken because I wanted him to remember me well. Everything was mediated by screens and we hovered, liminal, somewhere between the public and the private, somewhere between life and death.

My fingers grew stiff from hours spent gripping the sides of the magic rectangle that was a portal to this other, sterile world. The rest of the family rang in or recorded voice notes to say goodbye and I held my phone up to the iPad to play them, all of us at the mercy of these cold digital messengers. The only sign that he could hear us came when we tried to play his favourite Benny Goodman record down the line and I was sure I saw him wince. It must have sounded terrible refracted through two sets of tiny speakers.

Fixed to the image of my father I thought often of the double meaning of 'to screen': how it means both to conceal and to reveal. What I saw was reality, but edited by the boundaries of the frame. It was the truth and it was only a version of the truth. Just as I was with him but not with him, just as he was alive but not alive.

He died, as often happens, in a rare moment alone. The iPad battery ran out just as the afternoon's bad weather broke and rays of sun pushed through the grey. We paused our vigil to recharge the machine and get some air in the last of the daylight. After a short walk, on a strong instinct I rang the nurse, who told me she'd just been with him and there was no change, but to put my mind at rest she'd go back to check. Oh my dear, she said softly as she stepped into his room. She told me his skin was still warm. I had felt it, not in any of the places we usually put feelings – the bones or the guts – but in something at once far smaller and far more total. I felt his death in my molecules, as if in every cell I knew.

My father died and I kept on living, astonished by how simple it was to do. Each morning I woke up and each night I went to bed. I ate when people said I should and kept cracking glasses doing the washing up. I put flowers in vases and when they died I put flowers in the bin. Lit candles, lost my keys, and all my strong opinions.

After so many years of gradual loss it's hard to describe the shock of his absence, the intensity of it. Like the void, it was empty and full at the same time. The loudest kind of silence. The days and weeks that followed were a strangely sacred time. The present had never burned so brightly and I moved through it alive to the heartbeat in every living thing. My body was electric with feeling, I felt skinless but charged with a strength and clarity that surprised me. The worst had happened and I was still there, not careening towards oblivion but with my feet on the ground, rooted, able to withstand it. It was different but not worse than what had come before, and I didn't want to escape it because folded into the pain, the deep sadness and shock and mind-bending finality, was something infinite. Something that went beyond the limits of mortality and the rules of space and time. At the molten heart of my grief was the single greatest force in the fight against oblivion. At the centre of it all was love.

If you consider yourself a recovering alcoholic, the story you can tell yourself is one of resilience. When I was younger the freedom I wanted was to do with escaping my own mind. Now, I find freedom in knowing it. My recovery continues day by day and I have learned to trust it. I accept the void and most of the time it leaves me alone. When it doesn't, I try to greet it like an old but distant friend, with curiosity and with grace.

We tend to think of grace as to do with smoothness, elegance or the divine, but I'm more interested in the ragged kind. Like perfection or completion, smoothness is a false ideal: friction is where you meet reality. Instead, I look to the grace of natural processes that prevail in spite of everything – the flowers that grow on a volcano, the skin that grows over a wound, the forgiveness at the heart of love, the generosity of time.

EPILOGUE

Nine months after my father died I returned with J. to Stromboli. It was the tail end of summer in 2021 and we were elated to be somewhere other than our living room. The hydrofoil on which we travelled to Ginostra was stamped with the word 'LIBERTY' in letters two feet tall. Beside it was a logo of a seahorse, yellow on blue, the same colours I remembered from the postal donkeys' panniers from all those years ago.

The tiny port was empty and we were the only ones to disembark. We stood among huge grey boulders under a hot Mediterranean sun and watched as the boat sped back the way it had come. I'd forgotten the weight of island isolation and felt a tremor of panic watching it disappear. It's so quiet here, said J., as he shouldered the biggest of our bags.

The grey-blue sea was flat and soft beneath the volcano's jagged heft. From its peak a thin plume of smoke unfurled in greeting. Hello old friend, I said in my head, as we made our

way up the path. After the steep zig-zagging climb, at the entrance
to the village instead of a German postman or a donkey or any
suggestion of life we found a sign written in black marker on
a piece of wood and fastened to a concrete pillar. It read:

Pasquale Giuffré – luglio 2021
il dolore più forte della mia vita non aver potuto stringere
la mano di mia madre al momento dell'ultimo respire

The greatest pain of my life, I translated haltingly out loud, was
not being able to hold my mother's hand at the moment of her
last breath.

That Covid had reached even these remote shores was a sharp
reminder that the volcano was not an alternate reality after all.
For a moment my own breath was hard to find, but before either
of us could say a word the landlady of our bed and breakfast
appeared over the empty cobbles, waving with both of her arms.
Using a mixture of Spanish, Italian and Google translate,
Antonietta told us that we'd come so late in the season that
nearly everyone had gone. Apart from the place that sold dried
things, everything else was closed. Even the fresh produce shop,
she said with a grimace, adding that she hoped it would open
again in the next couple of days. I looked over at J. and could
see that so did he.

On our way to the apartment we passed bins that hadn't been
emptied for weeks. Stuffed black bags piled up like fake rocks
and baked in the sun, heaving with flies and a thick stench that
stuck to the back of the throat. With another grimace Antonietta

gestured at them and said, They no more collect! Everything broken.

Still, there was the blue of the sea and the blue of the sky, and the two nearest islands that sloped out of the water like whales coming up for air. There were the curly vines heavy with grapes, the limes and passion fruit about to ripen. Black dust, white walls, our tiny open-air kitchen. The weighted presence of the volcano. I'm sorry everything's closed, I said as we unpacked our things. I thought the season ended in October. It was always going to be a bit like this, said J., coming back. Sometimes an island paradise is really just a moment in time.

At the only open shop we bought olives and coffee, salted crackers, dried pasta and pesto made from local capers. It was delicious but not something you want to eat for six meals in a row. On our walks around the island we passed countless For Sale signs. The boats that came and went were bigger than I remembered, but it was rare that anyone got off. Instead of people we made friends with the island cats, lithe grey tabbies and ginger toms with golden eyes. Occasionally someone else would arrive in the square with a hopeful expression and an empty egg box but with Alimentari da Rosita closed no one gathered for a sunset *aperitivo*.

The third day we woke into a silence that was really full of sounds – crickets, strains of football from a distant television, a growling that was either feline or volcanic – but which, we couldn't quite be sure. A gang of swallows chased the flies from the bins, rushing from rooftop to rooftop before swooping out over the sea. Whenever I hear the birdsong I keep thinking it's the alarm on your phone, said J. That's how you know you're posthuman, I replied. Volcanic dust coated everything and I realised, in spite of ourselves, we had finally surrendered to the island. A butterfly danced over the vines.

As if that was all it took, that morning Rosita's was open. We bought fresh ricotta and bread, lettuce and fennel and Stromboli eggs. Yellow peppers and tomatoes of the richest red, long-life milk, tuna and chocolate. We ate lunch like happy emperors looking out at two white boats, their sails down, sugar cubes floating in the distance. Beside me, J. was reading a book about how to do nothing. My eyes were filled with blues and the blues were on my mind. It astonished me that after living through blues so dense they could have been made of rock, great chunks of lapis lazuli, there might follow lighter ones, translucent blues you can see right through, pale blues that dazzle. I was here and it was different and the same, and I was different and the same. Loosened by loss, no longer trying to escape myself, just another visitor passing through.

On the table in front of me the pages of my new green notebook were dotted with flecks of black dust. I could hear the patter of volcanic debris landing on top of the bamboo veranda. Bright sunshine caught the strands of white and silver in my hair. I took a caper berry from the bowl by my elbow and split it open with my thumb to look at all the seeds inside. Long in the distance, the horizon was a glistening boundary at the edge of a calm, reflective sea. I kissed J., picked up my notebook and went to walk up the side of the volcano. Perhaps later, I would write someone a letter.